How To Be A
Camp Counsellor

How To Be A
Camp Counsellor

... the best job in the world!

by

M. Catherine D. Ross

2005 Toronto, Canada

Published in 2005 by the Ontario Camping Association,
250 Merton Street, Suite 403, Toronto, Ontario M4S 1B1
E-mail: info@ontariocamps.ca • www.ontariocamps.ca

Library and Archives Canada Cataloguing in Publication

Ross, M. Catherine D., 1941-
    How to be a camp counsellor : ...the best job in the world! / by M. Catherine D. Ross.

Includes bibliographical references.
ISBN 0-9736987-0-5

1. Camp counselors. I. Ontario Camping Association II. Title.

GV198.C6R68 2005   796.54   C2004-906784-2

Funding for this project provided by the Legacy Fund of the Ontario Camping Association.

Cover and text Design: Karen Petherick, Intuitive Design International Ltd.
Consulting: Abbeyfield Consultant

Printed and Bound in Canada

Dedication

To all camp counsellors
who strive to make the camp experience
safer, better and happier
for every camper in their care.

Table of Contents

About the Book

The purpose of this book is to provide the information and tools to meet the challenges of the most exciting and rewarding job a young person can have – a job as a camp counsellor. Most of the time, counselling is such fun that staff don't even think of it as work!

All camps and campers are unique, but the role of the counsellor in any camp has more similarities than differences. Each chapter contains specific steps for dealing with many situations encountered in a counsellor's ordinary and extra-ordinary days. Resident camp counsellors can skip the chapter written specifically for their day camp colleagues, who can miss the section on bedtime routines. There are some sections dealing with serious problems that I hope you will never have to use. A detailed table of contents will help you to access topics if and when you need them.

The text in italics describes actual events experienced by others and myself. I find that counsellors learn better and remember longer knowing that they are dealing with fact not fiction. The follow-up discussion evaluates what happened and in some cases suggests what *should* have happened.

Throughout the book, I have interspersed the use of male and female pronouns rather than the annoying he/she, him/her combinations. However in every case, the text applies to both sexes.

I am grateful to Brian Blackstock, President of the Ontario Camping Association, for suggesting this project. Brian recognized the need for a book to replace the *Camp Counsellor's Handbook* written by John Latimer and himself in 1984 that would include current issues and some topics unheard of at that time. Along with all the traditional skills, today's counsellors need to know about life-threatening allergies, anorexia, West Nile Virus, Privacy Law, Abuse Law and Police Record Checks, to name a few.

I acknowledge and appreciate the support of the entire Board of the Ontario Camping Association for generously giving their time and sharing their expertise: Brian Blackstock, Robin Squires, Dave Graham, Ellen Nash, Rob Carmichael, Alf Grigg, Anne Morawetz, Sari Grossinger, Bill Stevens, Rick Howard, Pauline Hodgetts, April Young, Patti Thom, Duncan Robertson and Jeff Brown. I am indebted to other camp leaders who also shared their experience or allowed me to read their staff manuals and camp forms: Don Bocking, Skip Connett, Michael Bakker and Larry Bell. Sari Grossinger was a helpful resource for the day and special needs camper sections. We all benefit because camping professionals model co-operation.

I thank Jane Langford, a former Camp Oconto counsellor and currently a lawyer with McCarthy Tetrault, for reviewing the chapter on *The Counsellor and the Law*.

Special thanks are owed to the brave young girl, a recently recovered victim of a school bully, who read the section on bullying and confirmed, "I don't have anything bad to say about what you wrote. It describes everything."

With the permission of Larry Bell, Director of Robin Hood Camps, and the assistance of Dan McBride, I accessed the Robin Hood photo archives. Many of the photographs that appear in the book are from this collection. The photographer is Jake Benbihy. The rest of the pictures came from my camera.

Susan Potter, Andrea Ross, Cheryl Ross and Brian Blackstock assisted by reading the manuscript and making corrections and suggestions.

Introduction

As part of my research, I attended a daylong training event for young camp staff at Seneca College, King Campus near Toronto. All the delegates were eager to start their summer jobs as counsellors in a variety of camps across Ontario. Many were first-time counsellors or counsellors-in-training. I asked this group, "What is your greatest concern as you begin your first experience as a camp counsellor?"

Most of their concerns centred on their campers, which is good. This indicated that their priorities were in the right place.

- *Will I be able to give my campers the best summer ever?*
- *Will my campers like me?*
- *Will I recognize the kids who need help?*
- *Will I understand my kids and know how they feel?*
- *Will I be able to spread my attention around the whole group?*
- *What if I get a really difficult kid?*
- *What if one of my campers gets hurt?*
- *Will I be able to keep my senior campers motivated and challenged?*
- *Will I be able to keep my three- and four-year-old campers interested and attentive?*

- *Will I be able to get my group to co-operate?*
- *How do I put a group of campers to bed?*
- *How will I discipline my campers?*

Some were concerned about their yet-to-be-tested leadership abilities.

- *Will I make the right decisions when I am on an out-trip and there is no higher authority to consult?*
- *How will I react to an emergency?*
- *Will I know what to do and be confident enough to take charge in everyday situations?*
- *Will I be prepared with lots of program ideas – especially on miserable weather days?*
- *How do I maintain my enthusiasm till the very last day?*

A few worried about staff relationships.

- *Will I get along with senior staff?*
- *Will I be an effective member of the staff team?*

In the following pages, I address all of these concerns plus others that these novice counsellors hadn't thought about yet.

Peter McMahon, editor of *OCAsional News*, the newsletter of the Ontario Camping Association, describes the influence of a good camp counsellor. "I often think how lucky first year counsellors are. I envy them sometimes – more than any captain of industry or politician, they have the chance to make a difference at the most crucial time and place in a person's life."

But camp counselling isn't all fun and games. Anyone who thinks that has never done the job. On sunny days, if you are blessed with a co-operative, harmonious cabin group, the job is a breeze. As long as *you* are fun, creative, caring, patient and skilled with your brain in gear, you'll be a great success and everyone will have an exciting time! But on a stormy night, far from camp on a wilderness campsite, crammed into a four-person tripping tent with one camper sobbing because she is afraid of thunder, another complaining that her bed is wet, and a third whining because she's lost her flashlight, you may wonder why you ever signed that contract! Sometimes, courage, wisdom, sound judgement and perseverance are required.

This book is written to help you in all circumstances to be the very best counsellor you can be so that your campers will have the best time of their lives.

PART ONE

Focus on the Counsellor

Getting the Job 1

CAMPS ARE AS VARIED AND UNIQUE as the children who attend them. They can be day or resident, in an urban or wilderness setting and offer speciality or general interest programs. Some are privately owned and operated for profit, while a Board representing an agency or religious group operates others. There are special needs camps for children with cancer, diabetes, learning or physical disabilities and camps that include special needs campers. Some small camps may register twenty children at a time while large camps can accommodate up to six hundred. Some programs are highly competitive while others focus on co-operation and teamwork. There are camps for the economically disadvantaged with fees scaled to income and others that advertise themselves as children's summer resorts with every possible activity and high fees. Your job is to find a camp that needs your skills and talents and that matches your interests, needs and expectations.

If making money is a top priority, you would be better planting trees, working in a factory, labouring on a construction site or serving in a restaurant with a reputation for big tippers. You may not make great money at camp, but a counsellor's job has many non-monetary benefits: enjoying the outdoors, working with old and new friends, access to camp activities, the satisfaction of teaching and learning from the campers and knowing that you have made a difference in the lives of the children in your care. When the day comes that you need to commit to a job that requires your presence fifty weeks a year, you will discover that the characteristics and skills honed at camp are very marketable: your patience, perseverance, flexibility and creativity and your ability to lead, to communicate, to be a team member and to relate to all kinds of people.

Camp directors write many reference letters for former staff aspiring to be teachers, doctors, lawyers or leaders in business. The skills learned at camp will positively influence your success at school, at work and in personal relationships for the rest of your life. What better preparation for parenthood is there than being a camp counsellor?

How do you find which jobs are available?

1. Talk to your friends. A director looks favourably on an applicant recommended by a current staff member. Your association suggests that you are likely to fit into the camp's culture.

2. Go online. Directors post openings on sites such as:
    www.workopolis.com
    www.jobpostings.ca
    www.aboutjobs.com
    www.summerjobs.com
    www.jobbus.com

www.jobsearch.ca
www.summercampstaff.com
www.campcareers.com

3. Contact Camping Associations to check their Web sites and job placement services.

British Columbia Camping Association
info@bccamping.org
www.bccamping.org

Alberta Camping Association
info@albertacamping.com
www.albertacamping.com

Saskatchewan Camping Association
saskcamping@home.com
www.saskcamping.ca

Manitoba Camping Association
executivedirector@mbcamping.ca
www.mbcamping.ca

Ontario Camping Association
info@ontcamp.on.ca
www.ontcamp.on.ca

Association des camps du Quebec
info@camps.qc.ca
www.camps.qc.ca

New Brunswick Camping Directorate

office@nbcamping.ca

www.nbcamping.ca

Camping Association of Nova Scotia

info@campingns.ca

www.campingns.ca

Newfoundland/Labrador Camping Association

P.O. Box 50846

St. John's, NF A1B 4M2

709-576-6198 F:709-576-8146

Canadian Camping Association/
Association des camps du Canada

info@ccamping.org

www.ccamping.org

American Camping Association

www.acacamps.org

International Camping Fellowship

www.campingfellowship.org

4. Visit your high school guidance office or college or university placement centre.

5. Attend a job fair.

Do your research

Before applying, you need to know enough about the camp to conclude that you would like to spend time there. Chat with friends and visit the camp's Web site.

Contact the camp and establish how you should apply. Some may have an initial contact form that you can download from the Web site; others will suggest that you submit a résumé.

A succinct letter tailored to a specific camp should accompany your résumé. Call the camp office if you are unsure to whom you should address the letter rather than resorting to, "To whom it may concern." Briefly mention why you are applying to this particular camp and what you have to offer. A personal touch is appropriate. "Ever since my first summer at Camp Trailblazer, I knew that I wanted to be a camp counsellor." The covering letter complements but does not duplicate your résumé.

Your résumé will include more details on your education, work and volunteer experience. Ask friends and family to read your application and offer suggestions for wording and content. A second opinion never hurts. The package you send should be your best effort and free of any grammatical or spelling mistakes or ink smudges. The director will make some immediate judgements based on the appearance of your application.

It is wise to have more than one application in the works. Don't bank on getting the first job you apply for.

Interviews

Most directors like to interview applicants in person, either individually or in groups. The group may be assigned a task or problem, then observed to see how the individuals interact. Phone interviews may have to suffice if a face-to-face meeting is not feasible.

Preparation for the interview

1. Learn as much as you can about the camp from friends, brochures, videos or the Web.

2. Prepare several questions that you would like to ask about the camp: the campers, site, history, program and policies. Write your questions down and take them to the interview. Your first questions should *not* be, "How much money will I earn?" or "How much time do I get off?" You will need this information before you sign a contract, but if these self-centred questions are your top priority, the director will not be impressed.

3. Prepare answers for some likely questions. The director will want to know about your previous camp experience as a camper or on staff. Even if you have never been to camp, volunteer or paid work with children (e.g., babysitting, coaching, Brownie or Cub leader, Sunday School teacher, school mentor), community service or working with peers or adults provides relevant experience. He will ask about your interests, skills and talents. He may present a scenario such as, "after your cabin cookout, your group absolutely refuses to wash the pots and dishes," and ask you what you would do.

Experienced interviewers have a talent for asking probing questions. Think ahead and be prepared.

- *What do you like about yourself?*
- *What is leadership? How do you recognize a good leader?*
- *What do you value the most? Why?*
- *Who is an important role model for you? Why?*
- *What makes you a positive role model?*
- *How have you contributed to a team?*
- *How do you deal with stress? Relate your answer to a specific experience.*
- *What are some of the issues in a child's world today?*
- *What problems might you anticipate with new campers?*
- *What would be a fun cabin evening program for twelve-year-old boys?*
- *Why did you apply to this camp?*
- *What can you contribute to make camp a success?*
- *If you could change one thing at home, school or work, what would it be?*
- *Why should I hire you?*

4. Prepare two or three references with contact information. First, seek permission from these individuals and make them aware of the positions for which you are applying. Choose objective persons such as: a teacher, principal, coach, Scout or Guiding leader or employer. Exclude friends, family members and your minister, priest or rabbi. Because the clergy are not free to divulge privileged information, an employer would not consider this an appropriate reference.

5. If you are hired, you will need a Social Insurance Number (SIN). The SIN is a nine-digit number used in the administration of various Canadian government programs. You require a SIN to work in Canada. To apply for a SIN, you must complete an application form, which you can obtain from your local Human Resource Centre of Canada or download from the Internet. You can then apply in person at your local office or by mail.

At the interview

- Arrive on time. If you are unavoidably delayed, phone ahead.
- Be neatly dressed and well groomed. The director will not expect you to wear a suit and tie (he likely won't be wearing one either!), but your frayed jeans and a baggy T-shirt are equally inappropriate. Some camps are OK with long hair on males, brilliantly dyed hair, piercings and tattoos. Other more traditional or conservative camps are not. If you want the job, know the camp's tolerance level and act accordingly.
- Greet the interviewer with a firm handshake (practise with family) and a smile (practise in front of the mirror). Make eye contact. Throughout the interview, maintain eye contact with whoever is speaking to you. This shows your interest and attentiveness.
- Look confident. Stand or sit tall with your shoulders back. Although you may be nervous, consider that you are not the only one trying to make a good impression. Should he want to hire you, the director has to present himself and his camp favourably.

- Bring paper and pen to make notes.
- Speak clearly and elaborate on your answers. One-word responses are not helpful. If you are unsure of an answer, take a moment to think.
- Be honest. Don't exaggerate your qualifications. A director needs counsellors who are self-assured not boastful and over-confident. If the job requires a higher level, the director will look favourably on your willingness to upgrade before camp. A standard statement in employment contracts reads: "Immediate dismissal may occur for misrepresenting information on credentials, qualifications or references."
- With your questions and in your answers, show your interest and enthusiasm.
- If there is anything to prevent you from fulfilling the job requirements as they are described to you, speak up. For instance, if you must have a certain day off to attend your sister's wedding, it is best to ask sooner than later.
- Be yourself. Camps need all kinds of counsellors on staff – quiet, steady, thoughtful, sensitive folk as well as the boisterous, active, cheerleader types.
- At the conclusion, thank the interviewer.

What are directors looking for?
- Someone with spark, energy and a positive outlook.
- Young people who feel good about themselves. Directors can teach you the necessary skills, but they can't change you. Allow your personality to shine through in the interview.

- Someone who enjoys working with children.
- Someone who is responsible and can make good choices.
- Individuals who are capable but not necessarily "stars." Star athletes or star performers may be more interested in their own achievements than those of their campers.

Job Contract

You may be asked to attend a second interview or you may receive a job offer based on the initial interview after the director has checked your references. If you have another offer pending or if you need time to consider, establish how long you have to make a decision. A verbal commitment is binding. If you value your reputation, don't reverse your decision.

The final step is signing a contract, the agreement between you and the director. Whether you are receiving a salary or working as a volunteer, the contract clarifies mutual commitments between you and the camp. In the case of paid work, it will state your salary with deductions and identify the method and schedule for payment (e.g., by cheque at the end of the season). By law, Employment Insurance (2.4% of salary) is deducted from all salaries while Canada Pension Plan (CPP) (4.95% of salary) is deducted from all employees over 19 years of age. CPP (QPP in Quebec) is refundable in your tax return if your annual employment income is less than $3,500. The contract states the duration (start and ending dates), time off and any benefits (e.g., assistance with transportation, access to medical facilities on site or room and board in the case of resident camps). Some camps allow you to take advances from your salary up to a pre-determined limit or permit you to charge certain expenses on account.

Contracts require you to abide by the camp policies. Some of these may be written into the contract (e.g., rules regarding smoking, alcohol and drugs). It may include a Code of Behaviour (see Chapter 3), which describes the expectations of your conduct. Read the document thoroughly and ask all your questions before signing. Both you and the director will sign the document to seal your agreement.

Police Record Check

At most camps, the hiring process includes a request to submit to a Police Record Check (PRC). This may be an expectation of the camp's insurance provider. Your job offer then depends on a favourable check.

There are two basic screenings available: one for a regular PRC and then a more thorough check for persons working with vulnerable, special needs campers.

Individuals may apply for their own PRC at their local police station by appearing with at least two forms of identification (one being a photo identification) and paying the appropriate fee if any (no charge for volunteers). Or they can complete and sign a Consent to Disclosure of Personal Information form, which the camp director then submits to the police service. Applicants under eighteen years of age must apply in person as they fall under the provisions of the Youth Criminal Justice Act. The record must be given directly to the youth who may then choose to share the information with the camp.

Although a PRC is not a guarantee of an individual's character or conduct, more camps are requiring this step to reduce the risk of hiring an unsuitable candidate.

Countdown to Blastoff! | 2

Pre-camp

Most camps schedule a mandatory, on-site, training period prior to the arrival of the campers. This is your opportunity to learn as much as you can about the camp's philosophy, policies and procedures, the campsite, the campers, the staff, your job and your responsibilities. Arrive on time for each session prepared to listen, ask questions and make notes. Be prepared to make suggestions and offer your ideas. However, avoid comparisons. Declaring, "At my old camp, we did it this way," implies that your old camp was better.

The director and senior staff will stuff your head with as much information and advice as time permits while stressing safety and fun – in that order.

Arrival Day

All too soon it will be time to put your skills, experience and pre-camp learning into practice – the day the campers arrive! You are excited and maybe a little apprehensive. Will I like my campers? Will my campers like me? Will I be able to give them a great time? Do I know enough to do the job well? Relax. Stop worrying. You can always ask questions and seek advice when you are unsure. You will continue to learn until the last day of the summer. In the meantime, have you prepared your campers' living space?

- Is your campers' tent or cabin clean, tidy and well ventilated?
- Post a highly visible, colourful Welcome Sign naming each member of your group. Be careful to spell each name correctly. This shows that you care and also helps the group to learn one another's names.
- Check that items such as a broom, garbage can and hangers are in place and that whatever equipment the camp provides for fire safety (bucket of water, sand pail, smoke detector, fire extinguisher) is available and operational.
- If the campers are sleeping on cots rather than immoveable bunks, arrange the beds so as not to exclude anyone. Be prepared for your female campers to rearrange the furniture. Either convince them that your arrangement gives optimum space or require that any changes must first have your approval.

Take a moment to recall how you felt on the first day of your first camp experience or what it was like arriving in a strange place or walking into a room knowing nobody. Now you are ready to meet your campers wearing your nametag and a wide smile.

The first twenty-four hours are crucial

- Greet each camper by name, correctly pronounced (ask if you are unsure). Check with your campers before using abbreviations or nicknames. Does Elizabeth like to be called Liz, Beth, Buffy, Betty or does she prefer Elizabeth?

I once made the mistake of calling a new nine-year-old camper Carla. Most young, first-year campers would hesitate before correcting the director, especially on the first day of camp – not this camper! With her hands on her hips and an annoyed look on her face, she set me straight, "My name is Clara not Carla. That is spelled C L A R A, Clara." I didn't make that error twice.

- If you are reading a list of names aloud, always check the pronunciation before beginning. Campers are sensitive about their names. An error usually results in laughter, which is embarrassing to the camper whose name has been mutilated. Check the spelling before you post a camper's name on a list or write it on an achievement card.
- Be present when campers choose their beds to ensure that everyone's preferences are honoured or fairly negotiated.
- Help your campers to move their luggage, unpack and settle in.
- Assist in erecting a clothesline for wet bathing suits and towels – not across a path and never at neck height.

- Describe the routine for the first few hours so that new campers know what to expect.
- Tour the campsite (point out all washroom facilities first!) with the entire group, both old and new campers. Former campers may object, but insist that they come to show the new campers the site or to explain some of the routines. Hopefully there is something new for old campers to discover. Keeping together initially helps to meld the group.
- Don't overwhelm your campers with too much information, but at least cover the most important rules to keep them safe on your site. The camp will post the safety rules for each activity so that campers can refer to them anytime.
- If you don't live with your campers, show them where your cabin is located so they can find you if needed.
- In casual conversation, get to know your campers. You may already have some information provided in advance by the parents or campers such as names of siblings, school grade, swimming ability, eating and sleeping habits, camper goals, parental expectations, recent changes in the family, fears and concerns.
- If one of your group is a former camper with a notorious reputation, try to avoid pre-judging. Allow the camper the benefit of the doubt. With luck, he has matured and changed for the better over the past eleven months. If you expect him to be trouble, he will sense this and deliver what you expect! Hopefully a fresh start with a new counsellor will result in a positive experience. If you do have difficulty with a camper's behaviour, seek help

from senior staff, but never discuss the problem in public.

· Find out early if there is something special your campers would like to do during their stay: perform as a cabin group on variety night, explore the nearby pond or go on a cabin overnight. Make every effort to schedule their wishes into the program.

First meal

Eating in a camp dining room is vastly different from meals at home. The number of people, the noise, the confusion, the menu, possibly even saying or singing grace will be new to your campers. You will need to show them where to sit, how the meal is served, how to get seconds and how to clear the table.

On day one, your campers may be too excited to finish a full meal, but on subsequent days, encourage them to eat a well-balanced diet. If the meal is served family style, it is your job to see that each camper gets his fair share. If your camper is reluctant to eat an unfamiliar food, urge her to try just a little. However, never force a camper to eat. I always remember the camper who insisted that oatmeal porridge made her throw up. Regrettably, her counsellor made her eat it and just as she said – up it came!

Throughout the meal, converse with your campers even if there is another staff person at the table with whom you are tempted to chat. You can learn what they enjoy most about camp, how they are getting along with their cabin mates, what their talents are to contribute to Variety Night or what their goals are for the session. Parents will expect you to encourage appropriate table manners.

First night

As you establish the bedtime routine, make your expectations clear. Don't give your group too much slack at the beginning. Later, when the routines are in place and everyone is co-operating, it is easy to relax the rules a bit. It is much harder to haul in the reins if things get out of control. If your expectations are reasonable, your campers will co-operate to get your approval. They want you to like them.

- After evening program, gather your group together. Keep them moving through the washing, tooth brushing, putting on pyjamas routine. Remind your young campers that a final visit to the outhouse or bathroom before bed is mandatory. With younger campers, it helps to have all the necessary items ready on their beds before evening program: pyjamas, toothbrush and paste, washing supplies, flashlight and cuddly animal. The more you can anticipate their needs, the fewer delaying tactics they can invent!
- Entice your campers to get ready for bed quickly by planning something special together in the time available before lights out. Campers of all ages love to have stories read to them. Pack some suitable titles for this purpose. Maybe your group likes to sing quiet songs, tell stories or just chat.
- In the time leading up to lights out, speak softly, calmly

but firmly. This is not the time for shouting, boisterous activity or horseplay. You want to gear your campers down not up.

- Make new campers aware of any strange night sounds such as loons, bullfrogs, owls or wolves.
- Have their flashlights available if they need to get up in the night. City kids who are accustomed to streetlights may be surprised by how dark the night can be.
- Reassure young campers that there is always someone on duty into the night. For older campers, this is a reminder that mischief will not go unnoticed.
- Campers rarely experience homesickness on the first night – they are too excited. Be prepared for this problem to surface a little later. (see Chapter 13)
- After leaving the cabin, remain outside quietly for a few minutes to confirm that your campers are settled for the night before handing the responsibility to the person on night duty.

In conclusion

Plan on devoting the first twenty-four hours (minus a few hours for sleep) to your new group. During this time, you will establish your relationship with them and their relationships to one another. They will quickly learn that the camp will provide their basic physical needs and you will meet their need to belong, to be accepted, to be cared for and to be loved.

- Your presence shows that you care.
- Your friendly smile says that you are happy that they

are your campers.

- Your enthusiasm assures them that camp will be fun.
- Your patience encourages them to ask questions and not to be afraid to make mistakes.
- By preparing their space, you give them a sense of belonging.
- By offering choices, such as how they will spend some free time, you are helping them towards independence.
- By speaking politely, you show your respect.
- By being a good listener, you encourage them to talk.

The Counsellor as a Leader | 3

Characteristics of a Good Leader

When you sign on as a counsellor, you become a leader. As one young counsellor describes it, "It's a little scary. You're not a kid anymore. You're the grown up, the one in charge." How well you lead will depend on your skills. Leadership skills improve with practice. Just as your campers will emulate you, you can learn from and imitate the leaders around you while developing your own style. Some leaders are loud, energetic, charismatic and love stage front. Others are calm, quiet, dependable and prefer the wings. All leaders exhibit certain qualities.

How well do you measure up?

- A good leader leads by example. She *shows* others the right way rather than merely telling them. She's the one *wearing* her sunhat and sunscreen.
- A good leader doesn't wait for things to happen. He acts to make things happen. He's on his feet helping a young camper to straighten his bed rather than lying on his own bed watching him.

- A good leader puts the needs and interests of others before his own. He willingly gives up seconds in dessert.
- A good leader can empathize. He puts himself in others' shoes and appreciates how they feel. He doesn't laugh when a novice canoeist dumps accidentally.
- A good leader anticipates and avoids problems. She hears the thunder in the distance and gets her sailing crew off the lake before the lightning strikes.
- A good leader doesn't ask his group to do an unpleasant task because he is unwilling to do it himself. He's the one scrubbing the greasy frying pan or the burnt tripping pot.
- A good leader remains calm in an emergency.
- A good leader makes sound decisions after careful consideration.
- A good leader inspires confidence in others.
- A good leader accepts responsibility for his actions. He doesn't blame others when things go wrong.
- A good leader encourages leadership in others and allows them to lead where appropriate.
- A good leader knows that leadership is about service, sacrifice and responsibility, not power and privilege.

Leadership Styles

	Autocratic	Laissez Faire	Democratic
Characteristics	The counsellor calls all the shots.	The counsellor lets the campers do as they please.	The counsellor involves the campers in decision-making.
Appropriate Application	When safety is an issue or during an emergency	When it is time just to hang out and relax	When planning programs, activities or cabin procedures
Implications	If used all the time, the campers will resent the counsellor and consider him too bossy.	Campers become aimless, bored and lazy. Campers need some structure and direction.	It is time consuming and requires compromise and negotiation, but it allows campers to grow.

A good leader strives for balance. Sometimes he gives specific directions to get the job done, while at other appropriate times he allows his campers to make their own choices and decisions. When you have to tell your campers what to do, speak in a polite, pleasant tone of voice to achieve the desired result. Regrettably, the trip leader on the portage in Algonquin Park had not learned this lesson.

It was the last portage of the day. Our girls' trip landed shortly after a boys' camp with young trippers. We held back to allow the boys to get over the portage first and avoid mixing up packs. I don't know if the male counsellor thought he would impress us with his macho manner or if he was tired and frustrated at the end of a long day, but he began barking orders at the young boys, "Hurry up! We don't have all day. Pick up those packs and get moving. There's no use whining or crying. Your mothers aren't here!"

This unpleasant memory still lingers after many years. I suspect some of the young lads on that trip haven't forgotten either!

You will leave your campers with memories for a lifetime – make them happy memories!

Group Counsellor

Your most important leadership role is counsellor to your group. You, more than anyone else, will determine the success of your campers' summer. You will exert tremendous influence through your close, personal contact. If you do your job well, your campers will have a great time and you will reap the satisfaction of being loved, emulated and remembered. As one camper explains it, "If you have a good counsellor, you will do anything for him."

Just Like You

When I grow up, I want to be just like you.
When I'm a counsellor, I'll make my kids
Feel like they're wanted because they're special.
I'll make them laugh when they don't feel like
  laughing,
And I'll try to make them feel at home when they're
  homesick.
I want to be a counsellor too, you see
Because you've made my summer so great.
Maybe, just maybe, some day I could make
Someone as happy as you've made me.

This poem, written by three ten-year-old campers to their favourite counsellor, is high praise indeed.

Never underestimate the impact you will have on a young person's life. You are responsible for the safety, well-being and happiness of each one in your group. Parents trust you to care for the most precious thing in their lives. Directors depend on you to give each child the best possible experience. They will give you all the training, encouragement and support possible to help you do an excellent job. Always remember, **Camp is for the campers**. Everything you say and do should be in their best interests.

Camps are usually organized in one of two ways: the group system or the activity system. In the first system, the group of campers makes program choices together then moves throughout the day as a unit with their counsellor. At each activity, their counsellor either leads or assists a program specialist. In the activity system, each camper makes his own choices then participates with others who made the same choice for that time period. He will meet up with his counsellor when he attends the activity that his counsellor is assigned to teach.

In the group case, the campers and their counsellor spend most of their day together; whereas in the activity system, they are together at key times: wake-up, meals, evening program and bedtime.

Either way, the counsellor has considerable opportunity to make an impact on his campers' experience. Your words and actions will be remembered for a lifetime.

Stephanie was a first time eight-year-old camper. Part of her hesitation about going to camp was because she would be away from home on her birthday. She was most surprised and pleased when the day arrived and her counsellor, Adrienne, whom she adored, gave her a small parcel. She unwrapped a copy of Johanna Spyri's classic, Heidi. Adrienne's thoughtfulness made Stephanie feel very special.

This happened in 1978. Decades later, Stephanie fondly remembers Adrienne and her camper days as she reads *Heidi* to her own daughter.

How can you lead your group through a successful summer?

Have fun!

Ask any camper why he comes to camp and the answer is simple – to have fun! It is your job to make each day fun from start to finish. Your enthusiasm, creativity and sense of humour will make this happen. If you are enthusiastic about everything (the food, the weather, the activities) not just the things you like, your campers will be too. Be positive about everything. Laugh *at* yourself and *with* your campers.

It's OK to be a little crazy. As one camper puts it, "Camp rocks because no matter how crazy you are, you know that someone will be crazy with you!" Pack your father's collection of old ties and dress your cabin formally for dinner in T-shirt and tie. Leave invitations to a marshmallow roast under your campers' pillows. Ask yourself, "What can I do with my group today that will be fun, exciting and a little off the wall?"

Howie was scheduled to take Melissa's eight-year-old campers on their first overnight canoe trip. Just as they were launching their canoes, thunder rumbled in the distance. Looking across the lake, they watched the rain approaching from the far shore. The girls' excitement quickly turned to disappointment. Looking at their sad faces, Howie announced that they had exactly ten minutes to return their bedrolls to their cabin and meet him in the lodge. He grabbed the hot chocolate and marshmallows from the food pack, made a quick detour past the costume cupboard and in ten minutes, Bozo the Clown burst into the lodge ready to throw an Indoor Canoe Trip Party!

Be safe

Fun is important but safety must come first. You have to *be there* at all times to observe and supervise your campers to keep them safe. All day as you change venues and activities, you are counting your campers. An attentive, alert counsellor anticipates and prevents problems. At the overnight site, he checks the water for depth and hazards before his campers go swimming. He moves the group back from the campfire before someone gets burned. He stops horseplay before a camper is hurt. A good counsellor always thinks before he acts and makes sound decisions. When unsure about what to do, he asks for help.

Be generous with your time

A counsellor's success with her campers is in direct proportion to the amount of time she spends with them. Younger campers want you there all the time. Senior campers will enjoy having you hang out with them, but at times, they will want the independence of being on their own. Be observant and respond to your campers' needs. Concentrate on your own group. Campers will be jealous if you spend time with other groups. Campers who get a fair share of their counsellor's time and attention will not have to engage in annoying attention-seeking behaviours. Give your campers your attention before they demand it. Of course, counsellors also need some time to themselves.

Listen well

One of the most important characteristics of a good counsellor is to be a good listener. Aim to talk less and listen more. No one in a position of leadership can ever listen too much. Respond to your camper the *first* time she speaks to you.

Begin by making eye contact with the speaker. With young campers, kneel or sit down so as not to appear overwhelming or intimidating. Acknowledge that you are listening by nodding your head and making brief comments. Don't rush the speaker. Smile and look interested and reassuring. Be patient with a camper who has difficulty explaining himself. If you don't agree with what you are hearing, avoid correcting, criticizing or judging. Don't offer advice unless asked. Allow the camper to figure out her own solutions. Let the camper finish without interruptions.

Communicate well

There are times when the campers will need to listen to you. If you are speaking to a large group, ensure that everyone can see and hear you and you in turn can see everyone. Stand while they sit or position yourself on a higher level to facilitate their view. Campers will get frustrated, become restless and start talking if they can't hear and see what is going on. Wait for complete silence before you begin. Initially, this may take some time, but the campers will soon get the idea. Most camps have a signal for obtaining quiet such as raising an arm. If you start while others are talking, you will have to keep raising your voice to be heard until eventually you will be shouting.

Before beginning, explain that you will answer questions when you are finished. Constant interruptions to respond to questions are annoying and you will quickly lose the group's interest. Aim to make your directions clear and complete to eliminate the need for questions.

After you begin, if a camper starts talking, stop, look at him and wait. Don't look annoyed. Simply smile and look pleasant as you wait. He will quickly get the message and be quiet.

If you want to keep a group's attention, you have to merit it. Be concise. Don't tax their patience. Be interesting. Use props and visual aids. Vary your pace and tone of voice.

Put your campers first

A good counsellor is always watching and listening so that he can identify the needs of all his campers. He is selfless and puts his campers' needs before his own. He serves them all the leftover dessert although chocolate cake is his own favourite. He reschedules his time off to be available to meet a camper's parents on visitors' day. He willingly offers his only pair of dry socks to a camper after four days of rain on a canoe trip.

Be SPECIAL –

Sensitive, Patient, Empathetic, Caring, Interested,
Attentive and Loving

A good counsellor loves each camper unconditionally. It is easy to love the co-operative, happy, keen campers, but for some difficult, rude, obnoxious campers this is a tall order. However, a caring, compassionate counsellor looks beyond the behaviour to the possible causes in an effort to understand the problem. If the challenge is too great, she seeks help. A good counsellor is empathetic. She can put herself in her camper's shoes. She can remember what it feels like to be a stranger in a strange place far from home. She can imagine how it must feel to be nine years old and wake up to discover that you have wet your sleeping bag.

Campers deserve an even-tempered counsellor. They will be confused by excessive mood swings.

Be grown-up with child-like qualities

The best counsellors are spontaneous, curious and never lose their sense of wonder. Encourage similar traits in your campers. Wake them up early to watch a sunrise or stay up late to wonder at the moon or stars. Take them on an exploration hike and heighten their awareness of the world around them. Allow them to experience the symmetry of a spider's web at dawn, the warmth of the sun on a rock, or the peace of a calm lake at twilight. It is not necessary to teach them the names of every tree, flower or fern but do teach them to look and listen. Try these games.

HUG A TREE

Location: a wooded area

Equipment: blindfolds for half the players

Campers play in pairs. One is blindfolded. The "seeing" camper turns her partner around several times to disorient her then leads her by a circuitous route to a nearby tree. The "blind" player takes a minute to feel the bark, the branches, the leaves and the diameter of the trunk. The players then return to the original spot. The player removes her blindfold and has to find her tree. Players quickly realize differences that they had been unaware of before.

WHAT DOESN'T BELONG?

Location: a wooded path

Equipment: any 15 items (e.g., elastic band, sunglasses, pencil, ribbon, etc.)

Before the campers arrive, the leader places the 15 items in the woods on the sides of the path within sight of a camper walking on the trail. Choose the items and hiding places based on how challenging you wish the game to be. The campers then walk slowly along the path and try to spot the fifteen articles. On the return walk, as you collect the items, the campers can discover any that they missed.

Variation: By using items similar in colour to the surroundings, you can introduce the concept of camouflage in nature.

THE SOUNDS OF SILENCE

In the outdoors, ask the campers to sit, close their eyes and be completely silent for one minute. Ask them to listen and raise a finger for each different sound of nature that they hear. After one minute, compare lists. Listen one more time to let the campers try to hear a sound that a friend heard but they missed.

Be steady and dependable but never predictable

Think of ways to delight and surprise your campers. If your camper does not receive any mail, write a letter yourself and add it to the mailbag. This will ease the disappointment until mail from home has time to arrive. If your camper loses a tooth, check if there is a camp procedure to follow or leave a note and a small gift from the Tooth Fairy under the pillow yourself. Surprise your campers with an invitation to join you for a cabin cookout or a paddle after dinner. At rest hour, deliver a supply of birch bark (from a dead tree!) to write letters home. Help your group to build a secret fort or tree house.

Be prudent

There are some topics that are not appropriate to discuss with campers. What you do on time off is your business. Impressing them with your adventures suggests that your time away from them is more fun than your time with them. Nor do they need to hear about your past experience, if any, at home and school with smoking, drinking, drugs or sex. If the campers badger you with questions, simply respond that these things have nothing to do with camp so let's move on.

Pace yourself

A counsellor needs boundless energy for a busy and active camp schedule – no more sitting in a classroom or in front of a computer screen all day and sleeping in on weekends. Particularly if you are counselling boys, your down time will be limited. Expect to rise early and be on the go for most of the day and into the night. Be prepared to participate *with* your campers, not to sit on the sidelines and watch. Counsellors have a tendency to burn themselves out before the end of the season. After putting their kids to bed, they are tempted to socialize with their friends till the wee hours. This is where your self-discipline kicks in. It is your responsibility to get adequate rest.

Don't gear down before camp ends. Make the end of camp as spectacular as the beginning. Plan an exciting event for the last few days to motivate yourself as well as your campers; then, everyone goes home on a high note.

Be willing to learn

Learning is a lifetime occupation. Whether it is your first, second or fifth year on staff, there is always something new to learn. Rather than fretting about a mistake, consider it another opportunity for growth.

If you don't know something, admit it. Then if needed, learn it. You can't be expected to know everything.

Be flexible

Working with children in the outdoors can be unpredictable. It helps to be flexible, tolerant and ready to compromise. Just when you are set to leave on an excursion, the bus is late, it starts to rain and one of your campers feels sick. A good counsellor is prepared with an alternate plan for inclement weather and a game or two up his sleeve to play anywhere at anytime. (see Games, Chapter 17)

Accept evaluation

A process for evaluation is the norm in most camps. Your performance may be judged on an ongoing daily basis, mid term and at the end of your contract. The camp may use a form for this purpose. It is helpful for you to know the criteria for evaluation in advance. None of us likes to be criticized, but then none of us is perfect – including the director! When it is time for the senior staff and/or director to evaluate your performance, be receptive rather than defensive. They will objectively describe your strengths and weaknesses and suggest areas for improvement. You may choose to set some personal goals in areas you know to be lacking (e.g., to become more comfortable speaking in front of a group or to be more patient in dealing with difficult campers). In my CIT evaluation a lifetime ago, my director gave me some sound advice, which I still remember and apply to this day.

Hopefully there will be opportunities for you to give feedback to the senior staff and director. If you are a new employee looking at the camp operation with fresh eyes, your input could be valuable.

The goal of good counselling – a camper's self-esteem

Self-esteem, how a person values himself, is the key to success. It facilitates learning, growth and development. Campers with a positive self-image, who feel capable, are eager to learn and to try new things. Campers who feel loveable and good about themselves get along well with others. They are better equipped to resist negative peer pressure.

A good leader promotes self-esteem by:

- Encouraging the camper to do what he is capable of doing – like carrying his own pack to the end of the portage.

- Allowing the camper to make choices and decisions appropriate to his age.
- Encouraging the camper to accept responsibility for his belongings and his actions.
- Treating the camper with respect.
- Listening with interest to what he has to say.
- Encouraging the camper to set realistic goals. If these include improving a skill, make the instructional staff aware.
- Encouraging his attempts.
- Praising his successes, however small. (see Chapter 6)

Code of Behaviour
The description of how a counsellor is expected to behave may be found in the staff manual or stated in a separate document.

A counsellor is always cool, calm and collected
Counselling is a demanding job that requires an unending supply of energy, patience and a sense of humour. Under all trying circumstances, counsellors are expected to be calm and controlled. To do the job well, you need to be fit, well rested and recognize your own limits. Use any free time during the day to relax and do something that you enjoy. Go to bed at a decent time. On your time off, get off the campsite for a complete break.

A counsellor controls his anger
Anger is a legitimate emotion that should be expressed, not repressed, *after* you have gained control. If your campers exceed the limits, you don't want to shout at them and say things that you will later regret. Before you explode, ask a fellow counsellor

to step in so you can take a break. If no help is available, take a deep breath and count to ten – slowly. For many, exercise is an effective stress-reliever. Seek the help of senior staff to solve the problem.

If you are ever tempted to lose your temper, remember Heather.

 Heather arrived at camp full of anger. She had suffered more in her nine years than most have to cope with in a lifetime. Her mother had died when she was very young. A few years later, her step-mother died. Now, her father's new partner had a daughter also called Heather. Unable to cope with all this pain, Heather was temporarily in foster care. Heather was angry with God, her father, her father's partner and the other Heather – she was mad with the whole world. When she took out her anger on her new camp friends by swearing and kicking, her counsellor took her aside for a long chat. A few days later, I saw Heather sitting alone on a stump in the woods, just off the path. When I asked her what she was doing she told me, "I'm cooling off the way Jess told me."

If Heather can learn to control her anger, so can the rest of us.

A counsellor is never abusive

Campers have the right to a safe, secure environment where they are cared for and respected. A counsellor's behaviour must be exemplary with never a hint of abuse or harassment.

Verbal abuse includes yelling, ridiculing, mocking, name-calling, swearing or sarcasm.

Physical abuse is slapping, hitting, punching, pushing, shoving, grabbing, dragging or tripping.

To avoid any allegations of sexual abuse, a counsellor should never touch a camper without the child's permission and never in a place normally covered by a bathing suit. At bedtime, rather than assume a camper wants a hug, ask her if she would like one. If a child is upset, ask if a hug would help. Allow campers privacy when changing and never be one-on-one with a camper in a private place.

Racist, sexist or sexual jokes have no place at camp.

A counsellor is always discreet

At camp, public displays of affection are not appropriate. All staff relationships, whether heterosexual or same sex, must be discreet. Camps have strict rules about staff sleeping in their assigned bed and nowhere else. Opposite sexes don't share tents on out trips.

No camp tolerates romantic relationships between campers and staff. Such behaviour is grounds for immediate dismissal.

In conclusion

There is immense satisfaction in being a good counsellor. You are making a major, positive influence in the lives of your young campers who will remember you for a lifetime. Counselling is an awesome responsibility, but it is a shared responsibility. The director, senior and support staff and fellow counsellors are there to help you. A camp staff operates as a team. More on this in the next chapter.

In summary, the recipe for a great summer is simple: be your best self, be generous with your time, be safe and have fun!

The Counsellor as a Member of the Staff Team

4

Your group of campers is your top priority, but as part of a larger camp community, you will be working with other camp staff.

Relationships with other counsellors

1. Be friendly with everyone. Beginning in pre-camp, get to know as many staff as possible including counsellors, senior and support staff. Include everyone in your conversations and activities. In pre-camp, deliberately sit with unfamiliar staff at mealtimes. If you are a former counsellor, avoid constantly reminiscing about last summer as this clearly excludes new staff. New staff should resist comparing this camp to a former camp. The statement, "At my old camp, we did it this way," is bound to set up barriers. Make suggestions without making comparisons.

2. Cliques and exclusive relationships undermine a happily functioning staff team. If you should develop a close relationship with one other person on staff, this should not be obvious to your campers, detrimental to staff relations or interfere with your job in any way.

3. Enthusiastically support your fellow staff members at all programs and activities. Your campers will emulate your enthusiasm.

4. If you have a disagreement with a staff member, try to resolve your differences in private. If this fails, take the problem to someone up the ladder who can arbitrate.

5. Avoid criticizing, complaining and gossiping. Such behaviour quickly destroys staff morale. Never criticize a peer in front of your campers or complain about another counsellor to your campers. If you have a legitimate complaint, take it to the person with the power to make the necessary change.

6. Share the workload. Nobody likes a lazy co-worker. Do your part to keep the staff lounge and your living quarters tidy. Staff cabins are rarely spacious. You may be allocated a space not much larger than your bedroom closet at home to live, sleep and store your belongings. An attempt at tidiness helps.

7. Obtain permission before borrowing *anything* and return items promptly. A missing lifejacket or only working flashlight can be particularly annoying. Some camps advise drivers not to lend car keys.

8. Support your peers by following the camp rules and policies. A counsellor, for example, who ignores the camp rule about not buying treats for her group on her day off, makes life difficult for those who do follow the rule. Counsellors in each section must agree to be consistent in applying the rules related to rest period and after lights-out. If one counsellor is too lenient and another too strict, trouble is inevitable.

9. Before leaving on time off, cover all your responsibilities. Relay any relevant information to the person looking after your campers.

10. Stay healthy. Eat properly and get adequate rest. If you are sick and confined to the Health Centre, another staff person will have to assume your duties.

To assist the support staff

1. Arrive on time with your campers for all meals and be positive about the meal. Serve all campers equal proportions from the quantity available at the table. There may not be more food available.
2. Make suggestions about quantities or selections of food through the proper channels.
3. Learn the system for requesting repairs to buildings or equipment.
4. Encourage your campers to express their appreciation for a particularly enjoyable meal or work done on their behalf.
5. Stay out of co-workers' space and allow them to get on with their work while you get on with yours. Don't borrow their tools.

To assist the program director (PD)

1. Offer your help to plan, prepare and execute special programs. If the program director asks for volunteers, get your hand up! Your campers will be pleased. "I like a counsellor who not only does a lot with his cabin, but is active in other parts of camp like doing skits in the dining hall or helping in a section program. He makes the cabin proud that he is their leader."

2. Arrive on time suitably dressed with the necessary equipment. Bring your campers, properly dressed and ready to participate, with you.
3. Participate with energy and enthusiasm.
4. Relay suggestions for future programs from your campers.
5. Encourage your campers to thank the PD for his work on a special program.

To assist the camp director

1. Do your best for your campers.
2. Know where your campers are and what they are doing at all times.
3. Keep the director informed of any serious camper issues. The director appreciates knowing about camper problems before a parent calls.
4. Ask questions and seek help – preferably before a little problem becomes a huge issue.
5. Treat camp equipment with care and teach your campers to do the same.
6. Follow all camp rules, procedures and policies.
7. Honour your contract. A director needs a counsellor who is honest and trustworthy, someone who adheres to his contract even when no one is watching, both on and off site.

The Counsellor as a Teacher 5

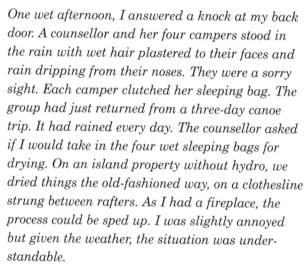

One wet afternoon, I answered a knock at my back door. A counsellor and her four campers stood in the rain with wet hair plastered to their faces and rain dripping from their noses. They were a sorry sight. Each camper clutched her sleeping bag. The group had just returned from a three-day canoe trip. It had rained every day. The counsellor asked if I would take in the four wet sleeping bags for drying. On an island property without hydro, we dried things the old-fashioned way, on a clothesline strung between rafters. As I had a fireplace, the process could be sped up. I was slightly annoyed but given the weather, the situation was understandable.

However, the answer to my next question quickly turned my annoyance to anger. When I inquired if the counsellor needed her bag dried as well, she replied, "No thanks. Mine is dry." This counsellor had failed in her key role as a teacher. If she could keep her own bag dry, there was no excuse for her campers' bags to be wet.

Sometimes counsellors, particularly those with young campers, are tempted "to do" for their campers rather than "to teach." Unfortunately, this counsellor failed to do either!

Good counsellors teach every minute of the day as they share their knowledge and experience. Each counsellor has a unique background and different skills to offer. Such diversity and variety enriches the camp experience for all. Knowledge that you take for granted and routines and skills that are as natural to you as breathing, need to be taught to your campers – simple things like how to address an envelope, safety tips like striking a match *away* from yourself or practical advice like inserting the match at the *bottom* of the fire. How to put on a lifejacket properly, where to sit in a sailboat, how to tie a boat securely to a dock, how to hold a paddle, where to find dry firewood after a rain, or how to tie a clothesline to a tree are simple or obvious to you but new to your campers.

At school learning is work; at camp learning is fun!
Campers learn happily and easily through doing and playing. The instructors, many of whom have recently been campers themselves, are closer in age to the campers and often know the campers well. Lessons occur outdoors not at a desk where you are expected to sit still. Campers are highly motivated because the activities are fun and they are learning something that they have chosen. Rarely is there a test or exam at the end of the course. The methods of teaching usually involve actively doing rather than merely observing.

Create a positive learning environment

A major obstacle to learning is the fear of failure. Children are afraid of giving a wrong answer, making a mistake or appearing stupid in front of their peers. The instructor needs to create a stress-free learning environment where mistakes are not cause for criticism – but gently corrected before moving on. Nobody (neither the instructor nor a peer) teases, disapproves or ridicules. The instructor makes only positive comments and allows only positive comments from the other campers. All attempts are encouraged, the slightest progress is praised and everyone is happy. If the counsellor expects the camper to succeed and tells him he knows he can do it, chances are he will.

Ten Steps to Effective Teaching

1. **Know the campers that you are instructing**
   Begin with an effort to learn the names of every participant. The more you know about your campers, the better you can adapt the lesson to their needs. Has David had swimming lessons before? Has Katie swum in a lake or only in a pool? Is Julie afraid of deep water?

2. **Help your campers set realistic, individual goals**
   A camper's goals should be achievable with some effort. At times, parents will suggest a goal for their child – to learn to sail or to pass their Bronze Cross. The counsellor should be aware of the parental expectations and encourage the camper in this direction but respect the camper's goals if

they differ dramatically from the parents'.

Encourage your campers to finish what they start. Each completed project does not need to be perfect as long as they have done their best.

3. Be punctual

The drama counsellor was late. The campers waited patiently for a few minutes, but soon became restless. Alex picked up a basketball and tossed it to a friend across the room. The catcher tossed it back and before long most of the group became involved in the impromptu game. The game came to a sudden halt when the ball crashed through a window spattering shards of glass on an unsuspecting camper sitting on the window bench. The counsellor arrived in time to carefully remove the glass from the camper's hair. Fortunately no one was injured.

Every activity, even drama, requires constant supervision. You can't guarantee the safety of your campers if you are not there. You should arrive before or with your campers. Your punctuality shows your respect. When the campers arrive, they will be eager to get started, not to wait and watch while you get yourself organized.

4. Be prepared

First *you* need to know the material that you are teaching and then you need a lesson plan, which includes the goal and method of teaching. Be sure all supplies and equipment are available. Teach campers to use and care for equipment properly. If a piece of equipment is accidentally broken, remove it immediately. Broken equipment is unsafe. Also if it is left lying around, campers may get the message that it doesn't matter if they are careless. Sailors need a back-up plan for windless days while canoeists and kayakers should plan alternate programs for when the lake is too rough. Everyone needs to plan for stormy days. Pre-camp is the best time to prepare alternate programs.

5. Be patient

Recall what it was like when you first learned a new skill. Some campers learn quickly while others require repetition. Some are auditory learners; others are visual learners. Their ease of learning will depend on their age and experience. Tell campers it's OK to make mistakes – it's all part of learning. Correct them and move on.

6. Be enthusiastic

If you are enthusiastic about your activity, the campers will catch your enthusiasm. Acknowledge the camper's effort. Praise a camper if he succeeds and encourage him if he has difficulty. There are countless phrases to encourage a learner: *good work, well done, keep it up, good job, great effort, terrific, fantastic, you're a natural, knew you could do it.* Add your own.

7. Have fun

> I hear and I forget.
> I see and I remember.
> I do and I understand.

Keep talking, reading, writing or memorizing to a minimum. "Demonstrate it" then let the campers "do it." When campers are actively involved and allowed to participate, their understanding, learning and enjoyment increases.

We remember about
- 20% of what we hear
- 30-50% of what we see
- 50-70% of what we repeat
- 70-90% of what we say and do.

Allow the campers to learn. On a cookout, let them do the cooking. It will take longer and the meal may not be quite as good as if you had made it, but the campers deserve to try, not just to watch! The message is simple. Children learn best by doing.

8. Be effective

- Reduce every skill to simple, doable steps. For example, a paddle stroke has many components: how to hold the grip, where to position your other hand, where to place the paddle in the water, how to move the blade in the water and how to return the paddle for the next stroke. Point out the campers' progress as they master each simple step. Increase the challenge with each additional skill. If you expect the campers to succeed, they will. *What you expect is what you get!*

- Adapt the lesson to the age and skill level of the campers.

- Make the best use of the time available. As soon as the campers know the basic safety rules, get on with the activity. Rig the sailboats and get out on the lake. You learn to sail by sailing, not sitting on the dock discussing theory or tying knots. There will be time enough for that on windless or rainy days. Better yet, incorporate a theory or knot-tying lesson while sailing.

- Explain the reasons behind the rules. When rules and procedures make sense, campers learn quickly and follow willingly: e.g., *You don't wear rubber boots in a canoe because if you dump, the boots fill up with water, they will be difficult to remove, and they will drag you down.*

Your goal is for the campers to understand and *apply* the rules, not simply to memorize them.

- Where possible, keep the rules positive. Campers like to know what they can do – not what they can't do: e.g., *Always swim with a buddy* is preferable to *Don't swim alone* or *Swim in the daylight* rather than *Don't swim in the dark.*
- Post important safety rules in a prominent place to allow the campers to see in addition to hearing the rules.
- Use words that the camper understands. A canoe may *dump* is preferable to a canoe may *capsize.* Every activity has a vocabulary that will be unfamiliar to a new camper: e.g., gunwale, bang plate, tumblehome or thwart. Be prepared to define and explain.
- At the end of the lesson, acknowledge progress and set a goal for the next lesson. Campers will leave feeling good that they have accomplished something even if it is small. Each success will build confidence and self-esteem. When a camper achieves a significant level, public acknowledgement will further boost his confidence.
- Maintain a record of the camper's progress. In following summers, after a quick review, she can continue to the next level rather than going back to the beginning. Don't assume that a new camper has no skill at your activity. Assess her ability and then fit her into the program at the appropriate level.
- Involve the campers in putting away equipment and cleaning up the area. This is a necessary part of the activity.

9. Be creative

Brainstorm with your fellow counsellors and make use of all available resources to come up with different ways to teach your activity. This keeps you from becoming bored as well as keeping the campers motivated. Theme days, games days, challenges, races, or special events will add interest and variety. Plan an archery tournament (dress as Robin Hood and Maid Marian to announce the event), a Guinness Book of Records Day or schedule a floating lunch in canoes. Let your imagination run wild!

10. Be alert

A good counsellor observes and eliminates hazards such as a nail sticking out of a dock or a broken limb hanging from a tree. He is aware of changes in the weather, such as a darkening sky, thunder in the distance or a sudden increase in the wind, and acts accordingly.

The Counsellor as a Disciplinarian

Megan is on night duty. One group of senior girls is giving her a rough time. Repeatedly, she climbs the steps, stands at the cabin door and asks them to please settle down. Her requests fall on deaf ears. The girls continue to chatter, giggle and defy her authority. Megan worries that when their noise travels to adjacent cabins, her problem will escalate. In frustration and desperation, she climbs the cabin steps yet again and shouts, "If you don't settle down immediately, you'll run around the tennis court until you are totally exhausted and ready to sleep!" By this time, the girls are completely wound up. They burst into laughter. Now Megan has no choice but to march them out of the cabin and up to the tennis court where they run around wildly having a wonderful time! Clearly, Megan's disciplinary methods are not working.

It is not uncommon for inexperienced counsellors to worry about landing in Megan's shoes. A question frequently asked in pre-camp training sessions is, "How do I discipline my campers so that they will do what I need them to do: tidy their cabin, get to meals on time, behave at the dinner table, co-operate with their cabin mates or get ready for bed?" First, let's be clear on the meaning of discipline.

The dictionary tells us that discipline is "training that develops self-control, character, or orderliness and efficiency." Individuals agree to follow rules and procedures so that groups can function happily together. Campers need structure and routines. They want and expect to be disciplined. In the words of a camper, "I like a counsellor who is strict but manages to control the cabin without us knowing it." If campers break the rules, then consequences, which are logical, fair and consistent, will follow. Erase "punishment" from your thinking and vocabulary. Punishment is all about laying blame and getting revenge, which results in anger and further aggression. The goal of all imposed, external discipline is self-discipline. Those who aspire to be good counsellors need to demonstrate a good measure of *self-discipline* before they can hope to control others.

A good starting point is to determine why the camper is misbehaving. You can learn this by observation or by talking quietly with the camper. They may be tired, hungry, sick or simply bored. They may not know or understand the rules. They may be seeking revenge for something done to them. Are they seeking attention, feeling powerless or overwhelmed by too big a challenge?

Avoid Behaviour Problems

Your best bet is to avoid behaviour problems in the first place.
How can you do this?

- Spend time with your campers, getting to know them.
  Ideally, spend a little time with each camper individually
  every day. Your campers are your top priority. Your
  presence tells them you want to be with them and that
  you care about them. Enjoy their company; encourage
  their efforts; praise their accomplishments and problems
  will melt away.
- Treat your campers with respect. If you treat them the
  same way you would treat your best friend or the way
  you would like to be treated, they will respect you in
  return. Respect does not come automatically with the
  title of counsellor; it is earned through your actions and
  effort. When your campers like and respect you, you can
  easily restore order without extreme measures when
  they misbehave. Speak politely. "Please be quiet" will
  get a better result than "Shut up!" Some counsellors
  erroneously focus on being popular. Respect has to
  come first.
- Show no favouritism. Although you may prefer some
  campers to others, their perception must be that you like
  them all equally because you treat them all equally.
  Chances are, the campers with the least appeal are those
  most likely in need of your help.
- Keep your campers constructively busy and active and
  minimize the opportunity to get into trouble. Most
  trouble results from boredom or inactivity. Help them to

set some high but realistic, achievable, individual goals. Be creative, enthusiastic and innovative in your programs. If cabin clean-up is getting boring, challenge the group to make their beds in sixty seconds with their eyes shut! Remember, however, they also need adequate rest. Overtired campers get cranky and troublesome.

- Try to anticipate and avoid problem situations. Be there to solve the little problems before they become big problems. If you expect fights over who gets the top bunk or who paddles stern, agree in advance to switch beds at the end of the week or change paddling positions on alternate days.

- Make your expectations clear. When expectations are clear, reasonable and achievable, campers will co-operate. For instance, after lights out, flashlights remain off, quiet conversation is allowed for fifteen minutes then everyone is silent and goes to sleep.

- Keep rules to a minimum. Explain the reasoning behind the rules. Where appropriate, allow your campers to set the rules. It is your rule that the cabin has to be kept reasonably tidy. Let them decide how they will accomplish this. A rule worth having is worth enforcing. If you are unable or unwilling to enforce a rule, get rid of it.

- Be willing to bend the rules when appropriate. It would be a shame to miss the Northern Lights, a spectacular starlit sky or an eclipse of the moon because bedtime is 9:30 p.m.

- Praise campers for good behaviour immediately and often.

- ❖ Be specific. "You've done a great job making your beds."
- ❖ Be honest. Praise only when it is merited.
- ❖ Be unconditional. Praise followed by "but" eliminates the benefit of the praise."You've done a great job making your beds, but the floor is a mess."
- ❖ Avoid comparisons. "John's area is the tidiest in the cabin." This could promote antagonism.
- Some misbehaviour is best ignored. At times (rest period is a prime example) campers will engage in annoying behaviour for the fun of getting a reaction. If the counsellor ignores the behaviour, it may cease. However, stay on top of the situation in case you do have to intervene. The key here is to reinforce good rather than negative behaviour by giving your group attention and praise for behaving well.
- Maintain your sense of humour. Lighten up! Don't take yourself too seriously. Remember what it was like to be a camper.
- Be firm. Mean what you say.
- Be fair. Treat everyone reasonably and equally.
- Be consistent. If you let your campers away with murder one night because you are in a good mood but scream at them the next night for the same behaviour because you are tired, you will confuse them. Your response to their behaviour must be the same today, tomorrow and next week.
- Never hesitate to seek help and advice when you need it.

Back to Megan and her campers tearing around the tennis court in the moonlight. What might Megan have done differently to achieve a better outcome?

1. Regain control while you still can. Authoritatively state your reasonable request once or twice at the most. Campers need to know that you mean what you say. Megan's repeated requests were ignored. She waited too long. Nagging never works. Campers will stop listening.
2. Take action. Enter the cabin and stand quietly in the middle of the room. This usually has a calming effect. When the group is quiet, exit but continue to stand by the door for a few minutes. However, if your presence does not settle the group down, at least you are in a position to identify the leader or instigator and remove her from the cabin. The leader no longer has an audience and those remaining in the cabin don't want to be hauled out next. Talk with the individual calmly out of hearing of her peers. Never berate a camper in public. She will be tempted to answer back to save face.

As the following incident illustrates, when things get out of control, you may have to take action even if you don't know who the culprit is.

 In my first summer as a camp director, a particularly challenging senior girls' tent group defied the combined efforts of the senior staff to settle them down at night. These four close friends and former campers felt threatened by the change in ownership.

This was their way of resisting change and maintaining control. At eleven-thirty on the fifth night, the counsellors knew they needed help.

Just as I entered the section, one of the group yelled at the counsellor on night duty to, "F—- off!" My first reaction was to smile at the camper's unfortunate timing, but I knew I had to be serious. I stepped into the tent and gave my speech. "It's late and well past time to settle down. Also, your language is unacceptable. I have no idea who screamed, but I will give the speaker one minute to admit to it." I then stepped out.

I did not expect a confession. If I were the culprit, I certainly wouldn't confess! In whispers, I consulted with the staff on our next move.

After a minute, I returned to the tent. As anticipated, my invitation for the culprit to identify herself was met with silence. I then announced that I was removing one camper to spend the night elsewhere. I admitted that I only had a 25% chance of getting it right, but if I chose an innocent victim, they would know it. I shone my flashlight on the first bed on my left and invited Sue to spend the night in the Health Centre. Not another sound came from the group till the morning whistle.

A week later, we discovered the real culprit when Christine gave a speech at Chapel on the importance of friends and in particular, camp friends. When she mentioned loyalty as an essential element in a friendship, Sue, disgusted by her *hypocrisy, turned her in. I then asked Christine to apologize to the counsellor and explain to every senior camper that she was the one who let her friend take the blame.*

3. Remain calm. Never discipline in anger. Megan resorted to shouting. If you are totally frustrated and angry, get help from another counsellor. Improve your chances of success. Two against a difficult cabin group are better than one!

4. Think before you threaten a group or an individual with a consequence. You may have to follow through.

5. It is difficult to discipline campers that you don't know. You have possibly witnessed the frustration of a supply teacher who can't even address an unco-operative student by name while trying to regain control of a classroom. These were not Megan's campers. She could have sent for their own counsellor.

6. If you are nervous about your first assignment on night duty, ask your section head to be nearby if you need help. Before handing over the responsibility to the person on night duty, each counsellor should quieten her own group.

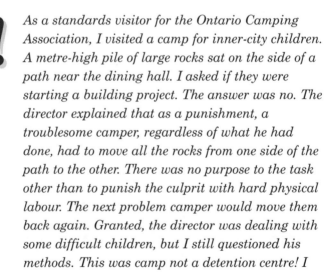

As a standards visitor for the Ontario Camping Association, I visited a camp for inner-city children. A metre-high pile of large rocks sat on the side of a path near the dining hall. I asked if they were starting a building project. The answer was no. The director explained that as a punishment, a troublesome camper, regardless of what he had done, had to move all the rocks from one side of the path to the other. There was no purpose to the task other than to punish the culprit with hard physical labour. The next problem camper would move them back again. Granted, the director was dealing with some difficult children, but I still questioned his methods. This was camp not a detention centre! I

suggested that he might get better results if he required problem campers to do something useful like build an outdoor fireplace for wiener roasts rather than waste their time and energy on a meaningless task. By giving them a worthwhile project, the camp would benefit, the other campers and staff would be appreciative, and the problem camper's self-esteem would move up a notch.

Consequences

Physical punishment cannot be tolerated. Extreme physical labour is as unacceptable as hitting, punching or slapping. Requiring a troublesome camper to stand outside in pyjamas to be eaten by mosquitoes is equally unacceptable. Depriving campers of food also falls into this category.

- The consequences of misbehaviour should be immediate, logical and reasonable. One consequence, hauling rocks, for every misdemeanour makes no sense. If a group refuses to tidy their cabin at the appointed time, what is the logic in cancelling their tuck for a week? Rather they should give up their first available free time to get the job done. If a camper sticks gum under his dinner plate, ask him to remove it. If a group sweeps all their litter out the front door, ask them to pick it up.
- Be firm but fair. The camper needs to understand what he has done wrong and why he is being disciplined. Your aim is to guide him towards self-discipline so that the misbehaviour will not be repeated.

- Sometimes all that is required is a look or a nod to indicate your disapproval.
- If this isn't enough, physically put yourself in the middle of the disturbance. A hand on the shoulder of the problem camper may settle the group.
- If further action is required, remove the culprit from the group for a short period of time. Speak to her quietly in private. Identify the problem. An older camper may be capable of suggesting a solution. Ask the question, "What would you do if you were in my shoes?"

Melinda was livid! As Senior Section Director, she was responsible for delivering campers' mail. One afternoon, the pile included an unsealed, folded note with the name on the outside of a camper whom she knew to be unpopular. Suspicious, she opened it. It was a vicious letter full of four-letter words signed, "someone who hates you!" As the intended recipient was away on a canoe trip, Melinda decided to act immediately. She gathered all the senior campers and announced that no camper would receive mail or tuck (both high on a camper's list of most favourite things!) until the culprit confessed. No one stepped forward. A prolonged silence followed. Melinda dismissed the group after urging anyone with any information to speak to her privately.

A day passed without a confession or any information. With each passing hour, the seniors became more disgruntled about the group's harsh

punishment for one person's bad behaviour. With
the intended victim returning the following day,
Melinda turned to the director for help.

Group Punishment – not a solution

Out of anger and frustration, Melinda had acted quickly and punished the group because she didn't know who the culprit was. Campers complained, justifiably, that punishing the entire section was illogical, unfair and only escalated the problem. And in this case, although we didn't know it at the time, the group had been falsely accused. Years later, we learned that the culprit was on the trip with the victim and had cleverly mailed the note before departing to divert attention and avoid discovery.

How could Melinda have acted differently?

If Melinda had taken time to think and had focused on correcting the situation rather than determining blame, she would have realized that the best solution was to destroy the note and say nothing. The intended recipient would be none the wiser and unharmed. The sender would not get the satisfaction of any response. Melinda would need to be alert to future attempts to harass the victim.

However, having boxed herself in, she went looking for help. On the director's advice, she gathered the group one more time and handed out slips of blank paper. She asked the girls to write down the name of the culprit if they knew it, fold the paper and hand it in. She explained that she would act privately on the results and that tuck and mail would resume. The director and

Melinda had already agreed that it was irrelevant whether a name appeared or not. The incident was now closed.

At bedtime, one of Rob's ten-year-old campers disappeared. He had sent the boys ahead to get ready for bed while he delivered their menus for an upcoming canoe trip. When he arrived at the cabin, seven of his campers were busy putting on their pyjamas, but he could not see Neil. The boys didn't seem to know where he was. Rob checked the washhouse and the nearby outhouses. He then retraced the path from the evening program site to the cabin, scoured the surrounding area and asked the other counsellors. Still no sign of Neil. He returned to the cabin. When he questioned the boys again, they averted their eyes, mumbled and shrugged their shoulders. Their behaviour made Rob suspicious. But, as twenty minutes had passed since he had last seen Neil, Rob told the boys to stay put. He was going to report to the director. However, as he opened the door, Neil's voice was heard above the boys' laughter, "Hey Rob, look up!" Neil was directly above Rob's head sitting on the rafters where he had been precariously perched the entire time.

Keep it in perspective

If you were Rob, how would you react? For twenty minutes the boys had fooled him and caused him some worry. Granted, they did call it quits before he involved the director. Understandably, his worry could turn to anger and he might shout, rant and rave at them about the risk of climbing the rafters and about his responsibility to know where they are at all times, which is difficult if they deliberately hide. If they can't behave in camp, how can he trust them to stay in sight on the upcoming canoe trip? They would go to bed feeling guilty and miserable.

Or he could take a deep breath, look at it from the campers' perspective as a harmless prank and in a calm, firm voice explain his worry and concern for them. Being absolutely clear about his responsibility for their care and safety, which includes knowing their whereabouts at all times, he could use the episode as a teaching tool and achieve a positive result.

Eight-year-old Jennifer is very upset. Her parents have just driven out of the parking lot at the end of Visitors' Day. She begins to cry. Martha, her counsellor, places her arm around her shoulder to comfort her. Her cries turn to sobs and her shoulders begin to heave. Gently, Martha tries to lead her towards a baseball game already in progress. Jennifer refuses to budge. She continues to sob, scream and hyperventilate, working herself into a full-blown tantrum.

Tantrums

Tantrums are more common in younger children. Because they feed off an audience, Martha's best option is to remove Jennifer to a quiet spot where she can sit with her and give her time to calm down. It is impossible to talk to or reason with a child in the throes of a tantrum. When Jennifer is quiet, Martha can ask what she can do to help. Jennifer will probably ask to go home. As this is not an option, Martha will apply the techniques for a homesick camper. (see Chapter 13)

Charlie applied every principle and technique in the book to succeed with his difficult group.

The director had assigned Charlie a group of eight eleven-year-old boys. She described them as a challenge. After three days of listening to them swear at, insult, tease, bully and fight one another, Charlie decided that they were "the group from hell!" Clearly if he and they were to survive the month, drastic measures were needed.

Charlie gathered the group and sat them in a circle. Speaking quietly but firmly, he established that nobody was having much fun. Together after some persuasion, they agreed on a code of conduct. They listed behaviours that were acceptable and others that were not. He explained that in the future if anyone stepped outside the boundaries of acceptable behaviour as agreed upon by the group, then he would gather them together again. They would find a quiet spot and remain there until they had found a solution that was acceptable to all.

It wasn't long before they tested the new rules. Quietly sitting in a circle, Charlie reminded them that it didn't matter who said or did what to whom. The misbehaviour was in the past. They were not

*there to assign blame. Their job was to decide how
to make things better now and in the future.
Eventually they resolved the immediate problem
and got on with the business of having fun.*

*In the days to follow, the boys had fewer fights.
They were beginning to have fun together. Charlie
was pleased. He praised his group for their
improved behaviour.*

*But on Visitors' Day, Charlie's counselling skills
were pushed to new heights! Ben, one of his
campers, was showing his mother his cabin and
introducing her to some of his cabin mates.
Unfortunately, the cabin did not meet this mother's
expectations for cleanliness and tidiness. In the
presence of his new friends, she remade his bed and
reorganized his belongings, all the while loudly
criticizing Ben for his laziness and carelessness.
Ben and his cabin mates were upset by her out-
burst. At that moment, Charlie walked in.*

*Introducing himself, Charlie politely explained
to Ben's mother that the group had a method for
resolving difficulties and invited her to join their
discussion. Suddenly at a loss for words, she
agreed. Before they were finished, Ben's mother
apologized for nagging at Ben, and the boys agreed
to make the needed improvements. Later that summer, the director received a letter from the mom
thanking Charlie for his guidance to her son and
showing her a better way to deal with problems at
home.*

In summary:

When should a camper be disciplined?

- when his annoying and disruptive behaviour is effecting others in a negative way
- when he refuses to respond appropriately to the reasonable directions from the leader
- when she tests the limits and exceeds the boundaries set by the leader
- when he is not pulling his weight and doing his share of tasks
- when he compromises the safety of himself or others
- when she flagrantly disobeys the rules

What should the counsellor do?

- Think first. Then speak and act. Remember, a child needs your love the most when he deserves it the least.
- Speak in a calm, authoritative voice.
- Listen attentively and objectively to all sides of the story. Find out why the camper misbehaved.
- Aim to solve the problem. Assigning blame and causing feelings of guilt are not helpful.
- Be firm, fair, and consistent.
- Be sure the camper understands why she is being disciplined.
- Seek help if you need it.

What should the counsellor not do?

- Never discipline in anger.
- Never berate a camper in front of his peers. Avoid insults, put-downs or sarcasm.
- Don't nag.
- Don't punish the group for the acts of an individual.
- Avoid idle threats. If you threaten with a consequence, be prepared to follow through.
- Never make false accusations.
- Don't allow one problem camper to consume all your time and energy. Your well-behaved campers deserve an equal amount of your attention.

Remember, the ultimate goal of external discipline is self-discipline. Some adults aren't there yet! Be patient and understanding with your campers.

The Counsellor as a Risk and Crisis Manager 7

During pre-camp, you will learn about the camp's Emergency Procedures, Risk Management and Crisis Response Plan. The goal of Risk Management is to prevent accidents. The Crisis Response Plan directs your actions should a serious event occur. Having a plan in place reduces "think-time" in the unlikely event of an accident. You may practise fire drills and perform underwater and missing camper searches. Ask if there are any modifications to the procedures if an emergency occurs after dark.

You will review fire safety procedures and safety rules pertaining to all the camp activities. You will practise first aid, cardiopulmonary resuscitation (CPR) and the Heimlich manoeuvre for choking. You may be taught how to use an EpiPen® for life-threatening allergies. If an emergency happens in camp, you will follow the instructions of the person in charge. If you are off site, you will have to rely on your own knowledge, experience and skills.

No one is sure how he will react in a crisis. Those with training in first aid, CPR, lifesaving or leadership skills will draw on this valuable experience. Once the adrenalin starts pumping, most individuals perform amazingly well, then collapse when the crisis is over. Your responsibility is to always put safety first and to be well prepared. But accidents do happen. Then, you proceed to do your best.

"I think I have chopped off my big toe and if I have, I don't want you to tell me!" Jill, the seventeen-year-old counsellor-in-training on our three-day canoe trip, stood in front of me, pale and shaking. An axe dangled from her right hand. The slice through the leather on her right boot suggested that her fear might be justified. As I was the senior counsellor on our trip with nine-year-old girls, she had hobbled to me for help.

Jill was an expert with an axe. As a camper, she had achieved the highest level in the camping skills program. Confident of her skill and motivated to help, she had borrowed the guide's axe without permission (her first mistake), moved to the edge of the campsite out of the way (good judgement here) and proceeded to split a cedar log (her second big mistake!). The camp rule clearly stated that on a canoe trip, only the guide uses the axe. Risk management had failed. I was now forced into crisis response mode.

Today, Jill has a nasty scar to show for her mistake. Fortunately, she still has both big toes.

When a crisis occurs

1. Pause, take a deep breath and proceed.
2. Summon help quickly – medical staff, camp director, fellow counsellor.
3. Administer first aid. Stabilize the victim. Seek further medical aid if necessary.
4. Attend to all present, not just the victim.
5. Once everyone is safe, decide the next steps to be taken.
6. Assign a recorder to document the action.
7. Give support to the leader.

Communication following the crisis

When an accident happens, it is essential that only the camp director or his designate releases information to the rest of the camp, the parents or the public. This is to prevent incomplete, ambiguous or inaccurate information causing confusion or further anxiety. Counsellors are advised to make *NO* statements or comments to the media.

Incident Reports

After an emergency or any unusual event, all involved staff should write separate incident reports while all the details are still vivid. Such reports are helpful to evaluate the situation and implement any necessary changes. These reports could also be useful if an outside investigation is deemed necessary.

Many camps will have a standardized form to record the following information:

- Date, time, location
- Person in charge
- Names of all present
- Weather conditions
- Circumstances leading up to the incident
- Description of the incident
- Action taken

The Counsellor and the Law 8

Duty of Care

When you sign a contract to become a camp counsellor, you accept the responsibility to care for your campers. In looking after them, you are expected to behave like a reasonable person – a person who is not perfect but who is certainly not reckless, ignorant or stupid. A reasonable person is neither overly cautious nor overly confident. If you have superior skill or knowledge in a particular area such as a National Lifeguard Service Award (NLS) or St. John's Ambulance Standard First Aid, you will be held to a higher standard than someone with no qualifications. Even if you are only a few years beyond childhood yourself, if you are engaged in an adult activity such as camp counselling, you will be held to an adult standard.

If your camper is injured while in your care (and there is no question that the injury was unintentional) and you and your camp end up in court, the issue for the court will be: was your conduct negligent? Was the incident an unavoidable accident or were you careless? Did your decisions and actions place your campers in unreasonable jeopardy? You are negligent if you do something a reasonable person would not do (e.g., persist in paddling across a lake in a violent thunderstorm) or if you fail to do something that a reasonable person would do (e.g., you forget to pack a first aid kit for your canoe trip).

Here are some simple rules to keep you and your employer out of trouble.

Be there!
Most lawsuits in the camp setting relate to inadequate supervision. The first question the court will ask is, "Was a counsellor present on the scene of the accident?" You can't look after your campers if you are not with them. This does not mean that you are in their face twenty-four hours a day, but it does mean that you must provide an appropriate level of supervision at all times. When your excited young eight-year-olds want to immediately explore the woods surrounding their overnight campsite, you should not be sitting by the shore taking a welcome break – you should be bushwhacking with them!

If an incident happens, report it.____
If Lindsay falls off the top bunk, even if she insists that she is not hurt, attend to it then report it. The medical staff and/or the camp director should make the decision whether follow-up is necessary. Your silence may cause more damage and could suggest that you are hiding something.

Know the rules. Understand and obey them.
If the camp policy is to portage around rapids, then portage. Even if the rapids are not very fast, you are behind schedule and the campers are complaining about the weight of the packs, you still portage. Think about it. If you ignore the rules established

by the senior leadership and an accident happens, you can anticipate that a court might say, "a reasonable person would follow
the rules." Rules are there for good reason. If you don't understand them or the reason for them, ask your director. But don't
take it upon yourself to ignore them when you are responsible
for campers.

If a camper says it hurts, it hurts.

Don't ignore a camper's complaint even if your camper is a
known whiner and you have heard the same complaint repeatedly. Follow up and get help. For one thing, your director may
have a solution for the incessant whining. But, more important,
you never know when the complaint is legitimate. No one will
remember the illegitimate whining if the complaint was real
and you ignored it.

Every party has a pooper and you're it!

When everyone is having a great time, someone (that's you) has
to step back, survey the scene and ensure that, in the enthusiasm of the moment, common sense and good safety rules are
maintained. If necessary, *stop* the activity *before* someone gets
hurt. Mud fights, pillow fights, food fights and general horseplay
fall into this category. At camp-wide regattas or sports events,
you must avoid getting distracted and caught up in the excitement of the competition and concentrate on your primary role as
a lifeguard or spotter.

Maintaining a calm and controlled environment is
particularly important in the dining room. Campers who are
laughing while eating can easily choke. Boisterous campers can
spill hot beverages on bare skin.

No means no.
Every child has the right to set his own limits. If a camper signs up for rock climbing then changes his mind when he stares up at the actual cliff, respect his decision. By all means, encourage a child to stretch his limits, but never force a camper to do something he refuses to do.

Everyone is entitled to bodily integrity and privacy.
Some campers are shy about undressing in front of others and this should be respected. Likewise if your camper appears uncomfortable with physical contact, don't insist on holding her hand, giving her a hug or sitting on her cot. Her discomfort may be a sign of sensitivity that can lead to misinterpretations.

For your own protection, never be alone with a camper in a compromising situation (e.g., behind closed doors in a cabin at bedtime or in a change room at the pool). There is safety in numbers.

Discuss before deciding.
At times, young counsellors find themselves in a position where they have to make serious decisions involving the welfare of others with little help. In camp, you can always turn to others for advice; however, on excursions or trips off site, you must make a decision yourself. At 6:00 p.m. on the second day of a four-day trip, an eleven-year-old tripper is complaining of abdominal pain. What should you do? High winds whipping across the lake and waves crashing on the shore are preventing you from getting your canoes around the peninsula to return to camp on schedule. What now? Take time to assess the situation, gather the information and discuss the problem with your peers and

the group. Consider what other sources of help may be nearby. After careful thought, do your best. If in doubt, lean towards caution. If you can say that you carefully considered your choices and can defend the one chosen on reasonable grounds, it is much harder to fault a mistake in judgement.

In all things at all times,
use your common sense and reduce risk.

Privacy Law

As of January 1, 2004, the privacy rights of Canadians are protected by federal legislation under the Personal Information Protection and Electronic Documents Act (PIPEDA). Camps must comply with this law by creating a privacy policy, informing the parents about their policy and training their staff to follow it.

A camp's privacy policy states:
- what information the camp needs to collect about its campers.
- how the information will be secured in locked files or in computers requiring a password.
- how the information will he used.
- who will share in the information.

You will receive basic information on your campers such as name, address, siblings, school and grade, interests, skills, eating and sleeping habits. You may also receive more sensitive information such as: *Ken's parents are in the middle of a con-*

tentious divorce. He has had a difficult year at school both social-ly and academically. He is a bed wetter. You are being given this information so that you will understand your camper's behaviour, be better prepared to meet his needs and support him to ensure a better camp experience. You will be reminded that this information is for your purposes only and should not be shared with the rest of the staff in casual conversations or with friends at home.

The entire staff may be given some personal information about an individual where a camper's safety is at risk. For example, if a camper is a non-swimmer, has epileptic seizures or is allergic to bee stings, everyone working with that camper should have the information, know who the camper is and how to deal with an emergency should it occur.

The Privacy Law affects you in another way. Campers and parents have the right and may ask to read any report that is written about the camper. If you are required to write camper reports at the end of a camper's stay, you need to keep this in mind. If your report is to be useful, it must be accurate and honest, but choose your words carefully. You may be tempted to write, *this kid is a loser,* but you must not! Be specific, fair and honest in describing his behaviour (e.g., *Tim has difficulty making friends. He consistently refuses to participate in the activities that the other boys suggest. He is a skilled, strong canoeist who constantly complains that his crew never paddles well enough).* Keep to the facts and allow the reader to form his own opinions and draw his own conclusions.

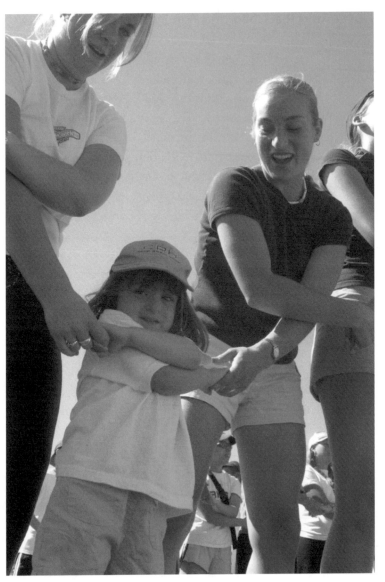

Abuse and the Child and Family Services Act (CFSA)

The CFSA recognizes that professionals who work closely with children (this includes camp counsellors) have an obligation to report promptly to a children's aid society if they have reasonable grounds to suspect that a child or youth under the age of sixteen is or may be in need of protection. The act specifically names youth and recreation workers as having a special awareness of the signs of neglect and child abuse (physical, emotional or sexual) and a particular responsibility to report their suspicions. Failure to do so is an offence and liable to a fine of up to $1,000.

The act states: *The person who has the reasonable grounds to suspect that a child is or may be in need of protection must make the report directly to a children's aid society. The person must not rely on anyone else to report on his or her behalf.*

Although by law you are the one responsible to report your reasonable suspicions, don't hesitate to share this burden with your camp director. Likely he has had previous contact with Children's Aid and can support you with this grave responsibility.

Physical abuse is suspected if a child has bruises, cuts, burns or fractures that are not adequately explained.

Emotional abuse is harder to detect. It involves rejecting, ignoring, isolating, or terrorizing a child. Children who are constantly yelled at, criticized and humiliated are victims of emotional abuse. "How can you be so stupid?" "You never do anything right." "Why can't you be smart like your sister?" "We would be better off if you had never been born." A child suffering from emotional abuse may be anxious, depressed, self-destructive, overly compliant and withdrawn. Conversely, she may be overly aggressive and demand constant attention.

Victims of sexual abuse may demonstrate an unusual and sophisticated sexual knowledge beyond their years.

The presence of one sign is not conclusive proof that a child has been abused. In most instances, abused children will exhibit a number of behavioural and physical signs.

Because campers develop a trusting relationship with their counsellor, victims sometimes disclose their sad story. If this should occur, listen sympathetically and calmly. Try not to show your dismay and shock and avoid making judgemental statements. Do not question the truth of the child's story. Don't ask the camper for details. Leave this to the professionals. Assure your camper that it is not her fault. Explain that you are obligated to report the abuse and ask the camper to come with you to the appropriate adult who can help you both cope with this serious matter. Report the disclosure immediately.

The Children's Aid Web site has additional information on this issue: www.casmt.on.ca.

The Day Camp Counsellor 9

Motivating Campers

Each morning, greet your campers eagerly with a big smile. For the first few days, be prepared for a few tears, especially from the younger campers. Be ready with energy, enthusiasm and an exciting program for a fun-filled day with them.

Your goal by the end of each day is to give your campers such a great time they can't wait until tomorrow. Unlike resident campers, every morning, your campers make a choice. You want them to eagerly choose to get on that camp bus because they don't want to miss a single minute with you and their camp friends.

Punctuality

Regardless of how late you were up the night before or how congested the traffic, you must be on time at the campsite or the bus pick-up location. If you become ill and are unable to go to work, you must notify the camp as soon as possible. The director and your campers are relying on you.

Parental Contact

Unlike your resident camp colleagues who may meet their campers' parents only once on a visitors' day, if at all, you could have daily contact with camp parents. The parents will judge the camp based on your appearance and behaviour; therefore, you need to be well groomed, alert, friendly, polite, helpful and informed. Likely you will be wearing a camp T-shirt and a nametag for easy identification. In conversation, enthusiastically share positive information about the camper, but if you are tempted to pass on criticism, check with the director first. He may have additional relevant information unknown to you or he may choose to deal with a potentially awkward situation himself. If, while talking to parents, you learn something of significance about the camper, pass it on to the appropriate staff.

At day camp, feedback is instantaneous. If a child goes home unhappy, the parent will know right away and phone the director immediately. Be sure to report any issues or incidents to the director *before* the phone rings. The director will appreciate the time to gather complete information and prepare a response. The parent will be reassured, knowing that the director is aware of everything that is happening on his site.

Security

Day camps have detailed policies to ensure that campers are released only to an authorized parent or guardian. Know the correct procedure and follow it exactly.

As day camps frequently share space with the public or are

adjacent to public venues, you must be diligent and alert to ensure the safety and security of the children in your care. Constantly count your campers. Be alert to strangers on your site. Approach anyone you do not recognize and escort him to the camp office. If you are unable to leave your post, direct him to the office and watch him as he goes. Report any person that you think is acting strangely. You can never be too careful when it comes to the safety of your campers.

When campers are on excursions off the camp property, they should wear a badge with the camp name and telephone number and a coin to make a phone call in the unlikely event that they get separated from the group.

Food Allergies

In camps where children bring their own lunch, extra care must be taken by staff to protect campers with food allergies. Everyone should wash their hands with soap and water before and after a meal or snack. Soap is needed to rid the hands of peanut oil.

Campers should not share food. If, despite requests to parents, a camper arrives with nuts in his lunch, without a fuss, the counsellor must ensure that the camper with the lunch containing nuts is seated at a distance from the child with the life-threatening allergy.

On the Buses

Bus safety

For many day campers, time spent on the bus to get to the site can be a substantial part of their day. It is up to the bus supervisors to make the trip safe, fun and rewarding. To reduce waiting time, leave the first few front seats empty. When the bus stops en route, the new arrivals occupy the front seats. At the next stop, the children in the front rows move back and the seats are occupied temporarily by the latest arrivals. This avoids waiting while children move the entire length of the bus at each stop.

- Teach campers always to approach the bus from the front not the back.
- Advise campers to remain seated, facing forward, with all body parts inside the bus.
- Keep aisles clear of equipment, feet and people.
- Staff are seated throughout the bus rather than sitting together at the front. In this way they can engage shy, lonely campers, spot any potential problems and assist with discipline. From the rear of the bus, a counsellor can view all the campers.
- Maintain a reasonable noise level that allows the driver to concentrate on driving and traffic.
- Maintain control at all times.
- Remind campers to take all their belongings when they get off the bus.
- If a child has to cross the road to her home, take her hand and walk with her across the street.

Bus Programs

A bus counsellor needs an unending supply of songs, quizzes and games. If the children are having fun, the time will pass quickly and inappropriate behaviour will be eliminated.

 ### Trivial Pursuit
Materials: quiz question cards
Divide the passengers into two teams. Pairs of players in turn are asked trivia questions. A right answer scores a point and the next pair on the same team is asked a question. The same team continues to receive questions until a pair gives a wrong answer. The questioner then asks the opposite team.

Theme Day

Choose a theme. Dress yourself and decorate the bus appropriately. Write a theme cheer and teach it to the passengers. Sing theme-related songs.

Multiple Words

Materials: paper and markers

Hold up a sign with a word containing many letters. Challenge the campers to create as many other words as possible using the letters from the one big word.

e.g., FANTASTIC contains over forty words – fan, fans, fast, ant, ants, sat, cast, an, as, tan, tans, tic, tics, fat, fats, fit, fits, cat, cats, tin, tins, can, cans, sit, sin, is, nit, nits, fain, tat, anti, antic, antics, cant, sift, stain, I, a, taint, taints, faint, faints, fist, saint.

Categories

Establish a rhythm to the count of four. Together everyone slaps their thighs (one), claps their hands (two) then snaps the fingers of their right hand (three) then the left (four). Once all the campers are clapping in rhythm, the leader announces with the snap of his right hand a category: e.g., flowers. Still maintaining the rhythm, the campers in turn call out the name of a flower with the snap of their fingers. No flower can be named twice. If a camper fails to name a flower as he snaps his fingers, he misses his turn and the next player changes the category so that the game can continue.

Story Time
The leader begins telling a story. Each camper in turn adds one sentence.

Humpty Dumpty Nursery Rhymes
Divide the passengers into two teams. Each team competes to see which can sing the first verse of the most nursery rhymes. Between rhymes both teams chant the chorus: *Hump-ty Dump, Hump Hump-ty Dump-ty Dump-ty Hum-ty Dump*. While one team is singing, the other team gets ready to start immediately without a pause as soon as the chorus is finished.

Famous People
Materials: blank slips of paper and markers, one container, a watch with a second hand

Players are divided in two teams. Each player is handed five slips of paper. On each paper, each player prints the name of a different famous person (real or fictional, alive or dead: e.g., Shrek, Shania Twain, Sleeping Beauty, Christopher Columbus and Mickey Mouse) then folds each paper once. The slips are collected from both teams and placed in a container.

The first player on Team One opens a slip of paper from the container and gives verbal clues to his own team to help them identify the name on the paper. He cannot use any part of the name in his clues. For example if the slip says Mickey Mouse, the player could say – cartoon character, created by Walt Disney, has big ears, eats cheese, etc. The team shouts out possible answers.

The player continues until the correct answer is given or one minute is up. He keeps opening more slips until his one-minute time is used up. The team scores points for each correct person identified. If a player is stopped in the middle of a slip, the paper goes back into the container for another player to finish.

After one minute, Team Two gets to play. The game ends when one team guesses the last name in the container. Compare scores to declare a winner.

 Travel Bingo

Materials: bingo cards with pictures in the squares (select pictures suitable to your route: e.g., a barn, stop sign, tractor, cow, church, garbage truck etc) and markers

Players mark the squares as they sight the objects en route. First camper to complete a line yells "Bingo!"

PART TWO

Focus on the Camper

Age Group Characteristics | 10

It is the director's challenge to assign the right counsellor to the right group. He considers the age, experience, skills, interests and personality of the counsellor and attempts to match these with a suitable camper group. He may permit his counsellors to choose which age group section they would like to work with, but assigning a specific group of campers is the job of the director and/or section head.

If you have siblings or have worked with children in other settings, you will have some knowledge of age group characteristics and be better equipped to make an informed choice. Having some understanding about how different age groups generally behave will help you to interact appropriately with your campers.

The chart on the following page describes some general characteristics. The best way to learn how a camper of any age behaves is to observe him alone, in a group, at work and at play.

Relationship to the counsellor

4-6 year olds	7-9 year olds	10-12 year olds	13-15 year olds
• Very dependent • Counsellor tells the campers what to do and how to do it . • Constant supervision is needed.	• Dependent • Campers need to know where the counsellor is at all times.	• Less dependent • However, the campers still want the counsellor's presence, approval and support.	• Counsellor is supportive. • Campers observe and follow his example without needing to be told. • He acts like a friend or older sibling.

Relationship with peers

4-6 year olds	7-9 year olds	10-12 year olds	13-15 year olds
• Tend to be self-centred • Tattle on peers • Play independently beside others	• Desire peer acceptance and enjoy group activities	• Enjoy group activities and need group acceptance • Individual personalities may hinder group cohesion • Like to be alone occasionally • Selective (cliquish) in choice of friends	• Seek peer support and approval • Have a few more permanent friends • Enjoy quiet times with cabin mates

Personality Traits

4-6 year olds	7-9 year olds	10-12 year olds	13-15 year olds
• Friendly, boisterous, helpful, curious, easily upset	• Inquisitive, energetic, active, trusting, increasingly independent, eager to please • Fear storms and the dark	• Reluctant to show fear • Fairness and following the rules is important. • Argue frequently • Beginning to question adult authority • Difficulty accepting failure	• Seek more responsibility • Sensitive to criticism • Want independence • Will form and strive for personal goals

Relationship to Program

4-6 year olds	7-9 year olds	10-12 year olds	13-15 year olds
• Activities are for fun • Short attention span	• Enjoy learning new things • Attention span of about 1/2 hour	• Keen to improve skills • More definite interests • Competitive • Hour-long attention span	• Seek new challenges • Enjoy taking risks • Will work to improve skill level

Your Campers' Health | 11

As a surrogate parent, you need to pay attention to your campers' health. As most of your campers will be in very good health, this is not a difficult task but a most important one. If your camper does have special needs, you will be told what they are and what your role is. Depending on the age of your campers, your role will be to cheerfully and repeatedly remind them to, "Brush your teeth." "Comb your hair." "Wash your hands." "Change out of your wet bathing suit." You must also make your own health a priority so that you will be able to care for your campers.

Providing for basic needs

First you must ensure that your campers' basic needs for food, water, warmth, rest and shelter are met.

Food
At mealtimes, by your own example, encourage your group to eat a well-balanced diet. If the menu includes unfamiliar foods or an item a camper dislikes, urge him to try a little – but never

force a camper to eat. Your positive attitude and enthusiasm for the food is the best way to get your campers to eat well. If a camper complains about a meal, politely ask him not to discuss the food before others decide they don't want to eat either. A camper may not choose to skip a meal without the permission of the health care staff. A camper on a special diet or with a food allergy may need extra attention. An allergy to peanuts can be life threatening. You will need to know, understand and apply the camp's procedure for severe allergies. (see Chapter 12)

Water

Particularly on hot days, encourage your campers to drink plenty of fluids at mealtimes and water between meals. When hiking and boating, remember your water bottles. Avoid heat exhaustion (symptoms include chills, light headedness, headache, nausea), which is the result of dehydration.

Clothing

Younger campers in particular will need guidance to wear proper clothing suitable to the weather. If left to their own devices, their raincoats and warm sweatshirts will remain in their luggage. Proper clothing is an important part of protecting your campers from ultraviolet sunrays and from insect bites. They will follow your good example.

Discourage campers from wearing wet bathing suits all day to avoid developing uncomfortable rashes. Urge them to hang up wet bathing suits, towels and clothes and then to bring them in before it rains.

Campers may need reminders to change underwear and socks or even to wear socks in the first place. Without prompting, boys would climb into bed in their clothes rather than change into pyjamas. Closed shoes are preferable to sandals to protect feet from cuts and stubbed toes.

Teach campers to wear clean clothing and put dirty clothes into their laundry bag. Mothers will not be impressed if every item of clothing beneath the top layer in the suitcase returns home untouched and unworn.

Rest

At bedtime, ensure that your campers are warm, dry and protected from insects. Provide an extra blanket on a cold night. If the weather is unseasonably cold, suggest that they wear a hat, fresh socks and a sweatshirt to bed. Young campers who are cold while sleeping are more likely to wet their bed. Towel their hair as dry as possible after an evening swim. Pull their beds away from the side of the tent or an open window on a rainy night and help them to put repellent on their hands and faces on a buggy night.

After campers go to bed, some or all counsellors remain on night patrol for two reasons: to ensure that the campers are safe and that they get adequate sleep.

Recommended hours of sleep		
Juniors ages 7 – 9	8:30 p.m. – 7:00 a.m.	10 1/2 hours
Intermediates ages 10 – 12	9:30 p.m. – 7:00 a.m.	9 1/2 hours
Seniors ages 13 – 15	10:30 p.m. – 7:00 a.m.	8 1/2 hours

Hand washing

Regular and thorough hand washing is the most effective way to eliminate the spread of illness and disease. Remind your campers to wash their hands before meals and after trips to the bathroom.

Insist on hand washing on out trips before the cooks start preparing others' food.

Sun Protection

Protect yourself and all your campers from too much sun. Campers who are fair-skinned, have red or blonde hair or spend a lot of time on the waterfront are most vulnerable to sunburn.

- Wear a full brim hat (preferable to a baseball cap) that protects the neck, ears and face, a T-shirt made from a closely woven fabric and sunglasses.
- Even in cloudy weather, apply a broad-spectrum sunscreen. Choose one that acts against ultraviolet A (UVA) and ultraviolet B (UVB) rays with a Sun

Protection Factor (SPF) of at least 15 but preferably 30 (the number means that it will take 15 or 30 times longer for the skin to burn). Apply generously thirty minutes before going out in the morning, after swimming or after exercise causing sweating. Reapply every two to three hours. To be effective, sunscreen must be applied to dry skin. Apply sunscreen before insect repellent if both are being worn. Wear sun block on nose and lips.

- Choose shade whenever possible. The peak hours for UVB radiation are between 11:00 a.m. and 4:00 p.m.
- Be aware of the increased exposure if the sun is reflected off water or sand.

Slip on a shirt – Slap on a hat – Slide on some sunscreen – Slide on the sunglasses.

Protection from insect bites

It is important to protect yourself and your campers from the discomfort and annoyance of insect bites. Mosquitoes are most prevalent between dusk and dawn and particularly annoying on windless, humid evenings.

- Reduce exposed skin by wearing loose-fitting, light-coloured long pants and a long-sleeved top. Tuck the bottom of your pants into your socks to protect your ankles, a favourite site for mosquito bites.
- A hooded sweatshirt has the added advantage of covering your neck. Mosquitoes and black flies love to

bite behind the ears.
- Apply an insect repellent containing DEET (N, N-diethyl-m-toluamide) in a concentration between 10% and 30% for children and not more than 50% for adults. Apply sparingly. A light coating is sufficient to do the job.
- Check that the screens in your campers' cabin are intact. If your campers are sleeping in a tent, close the tent before dusk.

International campers from countries where there are no mosquitoes have no immunity and are particularly vulnerable.

West Nile Virus can be spread to people by the bite of an infected mosquito; however, the risk of getting the virus is extremely low. Most people infected by the virus do not get sick, although a small number (usually the elderly and those with weakened immune systems) may experience mild fever, headache, stiff neck and muscle weakness.

Take the necessary precautions against insect bites so that you and your campers can enjoy living out of doors.

Medications

With the exception of an epinephrine (adrenalin) auto-injector (e.g., an EpiPen®) for campers with life-threatening allergies and ventolin puffers for children with asthma, all camper medications will be locked in the Health Centre and dispensed by the nurse. Campers who must keep their medication with them usually carry it in a fanny pack. You may need to remind them to have it with them at all times. If they are taking a prescribed medication, remind them to go to the Health Centre at the correct times. On site, it is not your job to dispense any medication, even an aspirin, to a camper. This is the sole responsibility of the health care staff. With direction, you may be asked to take on this role on an out trip.

Visits to the Health Centre

Changes in your camper's appearance (pale, flushed, glassy-eyed), appetite or behaviour (unusually quiet, has difficulty sleeping, disinterested, tired, whiney) might indicate a problem. If your camper complains of being ill or injured, always take him seriously and visit the Health Centre. It is not your job to diagnose. With the increased concern with the West Nile Virus and Severe Acute Respiratory Syndrome (SARS), campers with a fever or flu-like symptoms must go to the Health Centre. Even the smallest cut merits attention. It should be cleaned and covered to avoid infection.

If your camper becomes ill and has to spend time in the Health Centre, consider ways to help her recovery. With the permission of the health care staff, make a visit. Take a book, magazine or game. If she is not allowed visitors, deliver a letter. Suggest to her cabin mates that they make a get-well card in Arts and Crafts.

Head Lice (Pediculosis)

At some camps, the health care staff performs routine head checks when each new group of campers arrives. If head lice are discovered, one washing of the hair, combs and brushes with a special shampoo should solve the problem. The counsellor's job will be to discourage other campers from ostracizing or teasing. Head lice can affect anyone. It is not caused by a lack of cleanliness.

Adult head lice are very tiny, about 1 mm in length. The female lays eggs called nits that are greyish white, oval and cling to the hair at the scalp. Nits look like dandruff but will not easily flick off like dandruff. Nits are first found behind the ears, at the back of the neck or on the top of the head. Lice can survive only on the scalp.

Pay attention if another camper begins to scratch her head. This could be a sign of another case. Head lice spread easily, mainly by direct contact. They don't leap from one head to another. To prevent the spread of pediculosis, discourage your campers from sharing towels, pillows, hats, combs, brushes, hair clips or headphones – anything that touches the hair. Keep long hair tied back. Position beds to prevent campers' heads from touching.

If you are asked to assist with the treatment, follow the directions on the shampoo exactly. Most treatments use an insecticide to kill the lice and are only used when nits or lice are discovered – not for prevention.

Serious Health Issues 12

Laurie, a sixteen-year-old counsellor-in-training, arrived at the staff reunion party in December. In the five months since camp, she had lost some excess weight. Friends who had not seen her since the summer commented on how great she looked. She smiled. She was pleased that her efforts to drop those extra pounds were noticed. The following June, her parents drove her to camp to begin her job as a first-year counsellor. Walking off the dock wearing baggy sweatpants and a long-sleeved sweatshirt, she headed for her cabin. Her parents approached the director and explained in private that their daughter had not been eating well, but they were confident that because she loved camp and was happy to be here, her eating habits would improve. Before long, despite her parents minimizing the situation, the nurse and director concluded that they were dealing with an early case of anorexia.

Anorexia

Anorexia is an eating disorder, which affects 1% of teenage girls. Males are rarely anorexic; 90% of the cases are female. It is characterized by excessive dieting and a preoccupation with weight loss. In 10% of the cases, anorexia is fatal. Bulimia, characterized by binge eating and purging, although a more common eating disorder, is considered to be less serious.

A person is considered to have anorexia when her dieting reduces the body's weight to 85% of what would be considered normal. Anorexics eat little and exercise compulsively. Often starting in adolescence, it may strike athletes whose sport, such as running, rowing or gymnastics, requires a lean body. No matter how much weight they lose, anorexics still see themselves as fat. They wear baggy clothes to hide their skeletal bodies. Some cut their food into tiny pieces. Anorexics can be sensitive, insecure, highly motivated and perfectionists.

In the early stages, anorexia may go undetected because it is masked as a standard diet. Many deny their condition and resist treatment. Early detection increases the chances of a favourable outcome. At camp, you won't be dealing with a diagnosed anorexic. Hopefully, they will be in treatment elsewhere.

But, you *are* working with impressionable young women who are developing attitudes about themselves and their bodies. Dr. Gail McVey, a research scientist from the Toronto Hospital for Sick Children, surveyed 2,279 girls in grades six to eight. She reported that almost one-third, despite being a healthy weight, were currently dieting because they believed that they were too fat. Her research showed that one in four girls aged 12 to 18 in Ontario reported at least one symptom of an eating disorder such as having a highly restrictive diet, over-exercising, using laxatives or inducing vomiting.

McVey cites the media as playing a big role in influencing teenage behaviour. Magazine articles on the benefits of dieting, weight loss and exercise are abundant. Popular singers, actresses and models are always slender. The message to impressionable teens from the media and society is consistent and persuasive: thin is beautiful and results in popularity and success. Females grow up being complimented on their looks more than any other characteristic or quality.

To counter this one-sided barrage, what can you do to promote self-esteem and a positive body image in your campers?

- Be a positive role model by eating a balanced diet and encouraging your campers to do the same.
- Assure campers that weight gain is normal and necessary for children growing into adolescence. Often around 10 or 12 years of age, children pack on pounds just before an increase in height.
- If you are concerned about a camper's poor eating habits and/or compulsive exercising, talk to the nurse. But, keep things in perspective. For the most part, dieting in young women is a harmless and temporary activity.
- If you are trying to lose a few pounds, keep this information to yourself. Avoid comments such as, "I'd love to eat this chocolate cake, but it's full of calories."
- Comment on your campers' behaviour, personality and achievements rather than their looks. "Thanks for lending your backpack to Kim." "Your beautiful smile makes me happy!" "You did a super job pitching the tent. Co-operation works!"

Obesity

On the flip side, the medical community is becoming increasingly alarmed over weight increase in young people. Statistics Canada reports that about 35% of Canadian boys and 29% of Canadian girls are overweight and half of these children are obese. Young people are now experiencing health problems such as heart disease, high blood pressure, high cholesterol, and Type II diabetes that used to be confined to adults. It is estimated that only 10% of Canadian youth are active enough to keep their hearts in shape.

Dr. Brian McCrindle, head of the cholesterol clinic at Toronto's Hospital for Sick Children, believes that childhood obesity is a societal problem as well as a medical one. Ten years ago, all of Dr. McCrindle's patients at Sick Kids had inherited conditions that drove up their cholesterol levels. Today, all his patients are obese and their high cholesterol levels are the result of poor lifestyles: sitting watching too much TV or playing too many computer and video games, eating too much high-calorie, high-fat food and getting too little exercise. The alarming conclusion is that some children have become so dangerously heavier in this generation that their life expectancy is shorter than that of their parents.

Dr. Beth Abramson, a cardiologist and spokesperson for the Heart and Stroke Foundation for Canada has three tips for teens:
- Be active every day.
- Stay away from junk food.
- Avoid fast foods, especially in super-size portions.

Fortunately, the camp environment offers a healthy lifestyle to combat this problem. You can help your campers by:

- Focusing on healthy eating rather than on losing weight. Avoid mentioning weight or diet.
- Being physically active and encouraging your campers to do likewise. Invite them to join you for a morning swim or run.
- If the dining room is family-style service, serve reasonable portions. Don't offer seconds.

Life-Threatening Allergies (Anaphylaxis)*

*A condition of hypersensitivity to proteins or other substances, caused by previous exposure to the substance and resulting in shock or other physical reactions.

The girls were eating breakfast on the third and final day of their canoe trip. Andrea, an eight-year-old camper, was sitting by the campfire, spreading raspberry jam on her toast. A bee settled on her bare arm and stung her. Within moments, she was in obvious distress, complaining that she was having trouble breathing. Because the counsellor's younger brother was allergic to bees, she immediately recognized the problem. Shouting to the tripper to launch a canoe NOW, she quickly instructed the counsellor-in-training to stay put with the rest of the trippers. Fortunately, a boys' camp was located across the lake. They rushed to

*the front dock paddling as fast as possible while
reassuring Andrea that she was going to be all
right. She was, as soon as the camp doctor gave her
a shot of adrenalin. Knowing now that she had a
life-threatening allergy, Andrea would have to take
the proper precautions in the future.*

Food is the most common cause of anaphylaxis but insect stings, medicine, latex or exercise can also cause a reaction. Anaphylaxis is most often developed in childhood. If you have a camper with a known life-threatening allergy to peanuts or a bee sting for example, he must *ALWAYS* carry an EpiPen® in a fanny pack in the event of a reaction. An EpiPen® is a pre-loaded needle containing epinephrine (adrenalin) that can be used quickly in an emergency. An extra dose should also be readily available. Campers with life-threatening allergies should know how to administer their own EpiPen®. However, the counsellor must also know how to do this if necessary.

Some camps have eliminated nuts and nut products from their menus to reduce risk. However, it is impossible to guarantee a 100% nut-free environment and the suggestion of a risk-free environment has the potential to create a false sense of security. Constant vigilance is necessary.

As in Andrea's case, not all allergies are known. Anyone can have an allergic reaction at any time. Know the signs.

Think F.A.S.T.

Face:	itchiness, redness, swelling of face and tongue
Airway:	difficulty breathing, swallowing or speaking
Stomach:	stomach pain, vomiting or diarrhea
Total body:	rash, itchiness, swelling, weakness, paleness, sense of doom, loss of consciousness

Shoppers Drug Mart

Initially, the signs of anaphylaxis can be mild, but symptoms can worsen quickly. If a camper carries epinephrine, administer it immediately, then seek medical attention. If after ten to fifteen minutes the symptoms continue or worsen, administer a second dose of epinephrine.

Camper Problems

13

Bedwetting

Each morning, counsellors should discreetly check every young camper's bed for dampness, preferably when the campers are not around. Children who do not wet the bed at home may do so at camp because they are afraid of going to the bathroom alone at night. Be particularly suspicious if a camper's bed is made up first thing in the morning with no prompting from staff. If a camper is known to be a bed-wetter, the counsellor should talk to him privately in advance to assure him that together they will take care of the problem.

A camper who has wet the bed needs empathy, understanding and assistance. Confidentially, the counsellor arranges with the camper for the removal and laundering of the soiled bedding and pyjamas. Accomplishing this without the knowledge of the other campers reduces the possibility of teasing. If you are removing a camper's sleeping bag, replace it temporarily with a camp bag. However, if the cabin mates become aware of the problem, the counsellor should handle the issue openly and in a matter-of-fact way appealing to the others to be sensitive and understanding. Explain to the group that the camper will outgrow the problem, but in the meantime, there is no need to tease or make a big deal about it.

You can try to reduce the incidence of bedwetting by:

- reducing fluid intake after dinner.
- waking the camper and taking him to the bathroom just before you go to bed.
- making sure the camper is warm and cozy.

Homesickness

Six-year-old Becky arrived at overnight camp for her two-week stay. Although her mother had wanted her to wait at least a year, Becky insisted on going. It was the one thing she had asked Santa to give her for Christmas. Her three older sisters went to camp and she wanted to go too. Becky's mother did everything she could think of to prepare her for camp, including waking her up for the month preceding camp with the loud blast of a whistle! However, despite her mother's best efforts, her counsellor's loving care and the support of three siblings, Becky got homesick. She cried herself to sleep at night and woke up her counsellor at six every morning in tears.

Eleven-year-old Thomas travelled from England to Ontario for his first camp experience. He participated in the camp program for the first few days, but then he became homesick. All he wanted to do was sit in his cabin, look at pictures of his family and cry. When his counsellor urged him to attend activities, he refused to budge, repeatedly yelled "no" and clung to the rail on his camp cot.

Thirteen-year-old Emily had been at camp for six summers, but she still got homesick. When her counsellor asked her why she kept coming to camp, she told her that she loved camp so much it was worth being homesick once in a while.

Many campers get homesick at least once during their camp stay. Fortunately, with help from an understanding counsellor, the majority quickly overcome their sad feelings and soon become happily immersed in camp life. In my twenty years as a director, only one homesick camper went home prematurely and even she was writing to her tent mates within days telling them that she regretted going home and now she was "campsick"! The campers most likely to be homesick are those with little experience of any kind away from home or first-time and young campers, although campers of any age can experience a longing for home. It is harder for older campers because fewer senior campers are likely to be homesick and their tent mates may be less understanding. Children who are forced to come to camp or children with concerns about home such as a pending divorce or a parent who is ill are also vulnerable to homesickness.

The counsellor can help to avoid homesickness in his group by being particularly attentive at the beginning of each session. As your campers arrive, welcome them by name with a warm, friendly greeting. Help them to settle into the cabin and then tour the campsite. Show them the dining room, washrooms and where your cabin is located if you do not live with your campers. Describe the schedule and the activities for the rest of the first day. As the unknown becomes familiar, your campers will begin to feel secure. A camper may be fine for the first few days and then become homesick after the novelty and excitement of arriving passes or the first letter arrives from home. Be prepared with special activities for rainy or cold days to avert homesickness.

How do you identify a homesick camper?

A few homesick campers will weep and wail and beg to go home. Others are less obvious. Some may not realize that what they are experiencing is homesickness. Others will decide that they are homesick whenever anything goes wrong. A homesick camper may be unhappy, refuse to participate, choose to be alone, complain about everything and spend all her time with the nurse. However, don't jump to conclusions. The unhappy camper may have had a fight with her new friend. The child who refuses to participate may be afraid of failure. The camper who wants to be alone may simply need some peace and quiet. The constant complainer could be used to getting attention this way. A child who makes frequent visits to the nurse may have legitimate reasons. Get to the core of the matter by talking quietly with the camper.

What to do if homesickness occurs:

1. If the camper is crying, find a quiet spot away from the group and console her until she stops. Listen sympathetically to her concerns and feelings. Reassure her that it is normal to miss one's home and family and like other homesick campers before her, she will soon get over it. Assure her that she can always come and talk with you. Ask her what she thinks would help. For some homesick campers looking at family photographs, writing a letter home or receiving mail

from home helps, but for others, thinking and talking about home or getting a letter only makes things worse.

2. Talk about what she likes about camp. However, sympathetic conversation has its limits. You need to get the camper out and about.

3. Keep the camper busy doing something that she enjoys. Suggest suitable activities during the unscheduled times before meals or at rest hour.

4. Find a buddy to be with her and to play with her.

5. For a homesick camper, the end of her stay may seem like forever. Encourage her to try to be happy and enjoy her new camp friends and the activities for one day at a time. Focus on the things that she can change. She can't change the date of departure, but she can choose which activities to try.

6. Be particularly attentive around mealtimes and bedtime – times at home when the family is usually together. At meals, seat your homesick camper beside you. If she starts crying, try engaging her in conversation. Never send a weepy camper out of the dining room to cry alone. If she persists in crying, leave with her, have a brief, encouraging chat, go to the washhouse, wash away her tears, then return to the dining room. At bedtime, before saying goodnight, tell your group about a happy event to look forward to the next day.

7. If your camper persists in being unhappy, seek help from a more experienced counsellor or the director. Make all the staff aware of your camper's homesickness so that they can help her around camp. Inform the director of the problem so that he will be knowledgeable should a parent call after receiving an unhappy letter.

If you are patient, attentive and empathetic while keeping your camper busy, you will help her through this important stage of growing up – learning to be independent and happy away from home.

CAMPER COUNSELLOR JOURNAL

A counsellor can suggest to her homesick camper that they do something special together – write a journal. This activity will help to keep the camper busy and encourage her to think positively about camp. The counsellor explains that whatever the camper writes will be held in confidence.

Each day the counsellor writes a question in a small notebook and gives it to the camper who writes a response before returning it to the counsellor. The counsellor can add a comment then write the question for the next day.

Questions such as: *What did you do today that made you happy? Whom did you have a good conversation with today? What did you learn today? What's your favourite camp song? What made today special?*

If the rest of the cabin learns about this special activity, they too may wish to participate. Such a journal could be a cherished memento for any camper.

Staff Homesickness

When Allison, a first year engineering student, arrived at university, she stayed in a dormitory in the residence basement for the first five weeks until a room became available. The university had deliberately overbooked the residence knowing that space would become available when some students, who had never been away from home, were too homesick to continue.

Homesickness can occur at any time and at any age. If this is your first resident camp job and you have never been away from home for an extended time, be prepared for this possibility. Seek the support of senior staff and keep yourself busy. At some time, we all have to learn how to cope away from home.

Camper Fears

Children may fear things in the natural camp environment that are unfamiliar to them such as:
- *Reptiles and bugs that creep and crawl*: spiders, leeches, snakes or snapping turtles. Where leeches are a possibility, have salt available. Leeches appear as the lake water warms up over the summer.
- *Severe thunderstorms*
- *Swimming in the lake:* Some children, who are accustomed to swimming in a pool, worry because they can't see to the bottom of the lake and wonder what may

be lurking below the surface to harm them. With their counsellor swimming beside them, they may be willing to wear a mask and see for themselves what is under the water.

- *Dark nights*: Children are accustomed to night-lights in their bedrooms, streetlights outside their window and the beam of passing headlights. At camp, the night is dark except for the occasional flashlight, firefly or moonbeam.
- *Strange night noises*: The night is full of sounds that are unfamiliar to city dwellers: owls, loons, crickets, bullfrogs, quarrelling raccoons, creaking docks and lapping waves. Before saying goodnight, help your campers to identify the sounds around them and warn them of other unfamiliar sounds.

Acknowledge their fears. Don't tell them they are silly or inconsequential. To them, they are real threats. Teach them about the unfamiliar to help reduce their fears. Distinguish between what is harmless and what is potentially harmful. Then educate them to protect themselves against real danger. Reassure your campers that you are there to look after them and that their safety and well-being are your first priorities.

Some camp activities that campers fear can be eliminated or controlled:

- *Telling ghost stories*: Frightening campfire stories are not suitable for young and even some older campers.
- *Dumping canoes, sailboats or kayaks*.Lead campers through a controlled dumping. Explain or show them exactly what will happen. Reassure them that you will

be there to help and that they will not get hurt or stuck under or in the boat. Explain that there is an air pocket under a dumped canoe and sailboat. Don't force a camper to dump against his will. Be patient and empathetic.

Motivating senior campers

The director assigned me a group of eight senior girls with a sigh, "Do the best you can." They had all been at camp for years and were a tight-knit clique. At sixteen, they would have preferred to spend their summer in the city; however, their parents had insisted that they return to camp for their final camper year. They had no ambitions to be future camp leaders. They had done it all and were completely bored with every camp program. They arrived on Friday afternoon. Our first confrontation occurred on Sunday night.

Since time began, Sunday night at camp was Music Night. The entire camp assembled in the lodge for a program by the music staff. My group refused to go. Undoubtedly, they expected an argument, but I surprised them by responding, "Fine. Let's not. What would you like to do instead?" I had presumed that the director would allow me some flexibility with this particular group.

They were stunned. That was not what they had expected. Together we agreed to take our guitars, paddle down to the end of the lake, build a campfire and have our own music night. We sang and played for hours. They had a great time and so did I!

Some seniors can be difficult to motivate. Blasé and bored, all they want to do is hang out. Sometimes that's OK. During the school year, teens are tightly scheduled and under stress to do well. Having some time to themselves to wind down at camp is legitimate. Persuade them to take a short hike, paddle or sail to a destination where they can relax in the sun (well slathered with sunscreen) and read, write, listen to music and chat. A lazy afternoon spent fishing might have appeal. That way they get to do what they want as well as getting some activity and exercise.

Encourage them to make suggestions to the program director or to plan their own programs. Preparing and executing a Carnival Night for the entire camp would provide an opportunity for leadership. Giving them some control and ownership can be most effective in gaining their co-operation.

Staff Kids

Returning from a three-day canoe trip in the rain, Matt and all his ten-year-old trippers headed for the Trip Shed to unpack and air the wet tents and put way the rest of their equipment. All his campers, that is, except Drew. He made a beeline for the Health Centre where the nurse towelled his wet hair, wrapped him in an oversize sweatshirt and poured him a mug of hot chocolate. The camp nurse was Drew's mother.

Staff, whose children are on site in the care of a counsellor, can pose a problem. Some, like Drew's mother, extend privileges to their children that are not enjoyed by the other campers. Others interfere in the counsellor's role and appear at difficult times such as bedtime when a counsellor is trying to settle his group for the night. It is awkward for the counsellor to say anything because of the seniority or age difference of the parent.

This is one of those times when the counsellor might choose to ask the director for help. The expectations and policies should be made clear to staff with children on site. If they overstep the bounds, the director must intervene on the counsellor's behalf.

The Self-Centred Child

Only children who never have to accommodate to a sibling's needs or children with parents who over-indulge them may understandably become self-centred. They live in spacious bedrooms sometimes equipped with their own phone, television or computer. But at camp, we expect them to share limited space with several others. At home, there are numerous labour-saving devices and the demands on them are minimal – possibly load the dishwasher or take out the garbage – yet we expect them to make their beds, sweep the cabin, pick up litter and maybe at times cook their own food and wash their own dishes.

Fortunately most children want to be accepted by their peers and quickly learn to adapt to the demands of communal living at camp. They soon realize that life at camp means living closely with others, sharing their counsellor's time and attention and equally dividing up the one bag of marshmallows. By observing and experiencing the co-operative behaviour of the counsellor and her cabin mates, the selfish, self-centred child has the opportunity to learn to work and have fun with the group.

The Complainer

Occasionally, you will have a negative camper who complains about everything – the weather, the food, the activities, his cabin mates, whatever. Whether he does this unconsciously out of habit or knowingly for attention, it is annoying, demoralizing and contagious! Politely ask him to stop. Tell him you are not interested in his complaints, unless of course a particular complaint is legitimate. Challenge him to tell you something he does like. Ask him to make a positive suggestion. If he comes up with a good idea – implement it.

Theft

Most camps urge campers to leave valuables at home. If they do arrive at camp, lock them up in the office or other appropriate location for safekeeping. However, if a camper does report a missing item or accuses another camper of theft, proceed with caution.

Begin by helping the camper with a complete and thorough search of his own belongings and the surrounding common area. If the item is still missing, ask all the campers, in your presence, to join in the search, each one concentrating on his own area. Do not make any accusations. Simply explain that the item is missing and possibly by an honest mistake or accident, it has landed in the wrong place. If this extended search proves futile, suggest that the item may turn up in the future. If a cabin mate has stolen something, bringing the problem to light may persuade him to return the item anonymously.

If it is food that is gone, consider the possibility that a four-legged animal is the culprit.

Bullying

I asked a young girl who had recently recovered from a sad and frightening period in her life caused by the terror of a school bully to read the following section for accuracy. Her response is a plea to those working with children to be knowledgeable about bullying. "I wish I had this when I was going through a rough time. It would have been a breeze to explain myself. Now that I read this, I wish that the people who didn't come through with helping me had read it because they would have had some insight into what was happening."

Read on and gain that insight that could help your camper from the misery of a bully.

 Katie was a happy, friendly, twelve-year-old who was very excited about going to camp for the first time. She was tall and physically mature, but as she was socially immature, she made friends more easily with the ten- and eleven-year-old girls in the tent nearby. At times, her behaviour annoyed her

*own tent mates. During rest hour, Jennifer, her
counsellor, supplied her with comics and games,
but Katie quickly became bored. While the others
quietly read and wrote letters, Katie bounced up
and down on her cot making the springs squeak.
Katie had Attention Deficit Hyperactivity Disorder
(AD/HD).*

*One rest hour, after making sure that no
counsellors were within hearing, Alyssa, one of her
tent mates, let her have it. She told Katie that she
was stupid, useless and really annoying. For
Alyssa, camp had always been the perfect place and
she shouldn't have to put up with Katie ruining it.
Why didn't Katie just move in with her friends next
door? The other two girls in the tent said nothing,
but Alyssa, a strong leader, easily persuaded them
to exclude Katie from all their activities. Always
making sure that no counsellors were around,
Alyssa alternated between taunting and insulting
Katie then ignoring and ostracizing her. As Alyssa
saw it, Katie was spoiling her camp experience so
she would make Katie's time just as miserable.*

*Because Katie liked and trusted Jennifer, she
soon told her about the unpleasant treatment.*

Despite her best efforts to meld her group, Jennifer now knew
she had a bullying problem to solve. Often children don't tell
adults about bullying because they are ashamed or afraid of
retaliation from the bully. Alyssa, a popular, strong leader and
long-time camper who was concerned only about herself and her

perfect camp experience, was a bully. Katie, the new camper with a behaviour disorder, had become her victim. Melissa and Emily, the other two tent mates, played the role of bystanders. In the majority of cases, bystanders support the bully rather than aid the bullied. Typically bystanders are afraid of getting hurt or becoming a new target.

What is bullying?

Bullying is a conscious, wilful and deliberate hostile activity intended to harm, induce fear through the threat of further aggression and create terror. Bullying is not about anger or conflict. It is about contempt, a powerful feeling of dislike towards someone considered weaker, inferior or worthless. Bullying occurs most frequently with eleven- and twelve-year-olds. Bullies act singly or in groups. A child who is kind and friendly on his own can act like a bully in a gang. Bullies are often popular, intelligent and charming. They lack empathy, the ability to identify with and feel another person's concerns. They are preoccupied with their own wants and needs with no thought for the rights, feelings or needs of others. When confronted, bullies refuse to accept responsibility for their behaviour and make excuses such as, "I was just teasing." Teasing involves give and take and is enjoyed by both parties. Teasing becomes taunting when it is no longer fun for the one being teased. Bullies are intolerant of differences. Different translates to inferior.

Victims of bullying

Victims are campers who, in the opinion of the bully, don't fit in. They are chosen because they are different in some way: race, sex, sexual orientation, religion, physical attributes or mental abilities. The new camper, the smallest or youngest child, the overweight camper or the shy, submissive child are easy victims.

Three types of bullying: verbal, physical and relational

1. The most common form of bullying and one used equally by boys and girls is verbal, which includes name-calling, insults, threats, cruel criticism, gossip, false rumours, racist slurs or sexually abusive remarks (gay, fag, lez, homo, slut). It is sometimes hard to spot because the bully is smart enough to wait until out of earshot of supervising adults.
2. Physical bullying is the most visible and includes slapping, hitting, punching, kicking, biting, spitting or damaging the clothing or belongings of the bullied child.
3. Relational bullying involves ignoring, isolating, excluding or shunning the victim. Cliques that dictate who is allowed in and who is kept out are a form of bullying. A counsellor needs to be alert to such signs as: rolling eyes, sneers, snickers, sighs or campers who are laughing *at* rather than *with* a cabin mate.

Three elements in bullying, which are always present:

-   First, there is an imbalance of power, meaning the bully can be older, bigger, stronger, smarter or higher up the social ladder. Being a former camper, Alyssa felt she had higher status.
-   Second, the bully *intends* to harm and inflict either emotional or physical pain. The behaviour is deliberate.
-   Last, there is always the threat of further aggression. The bully does not intend to stop.

Fortunately, a safe and secure camp environment minimizes the possibility of bullying. At camp, counsellors are almost always around. There are firm limits on unacceptable behaviour and campers who violate the limits are consistently and fairly disciplined. When counsellors treat everyone with caring and respect and celebrate differences, campers learn to do likewise.

Steps in dealing with bullying

The camp policy must be publicly stated: ***bullying is not acceptable***. Prompt intervention by a strong, respected leader is the best way to eliminate it.

The Bullied

- Listen carefully and supportively to the details of the bullying. Take every complaint seriously.
- Reassure the victim that she is not at fault. The blame belongs to the bully. Even though Katie's actions were annoying, Alyssa did not have the right to make cruel remarks.
- Advise the bullied that ignoring the bully never works. The victim has to act. It does not help to fight back with insulting comments or to whine or cry. It is best to speak assertively, "Please stop it. I don't need to listen to this. I'm out of here." Then depart. It is best if the victim can deal with the problem herself. However if the bullying continues, she should report it, and the counsellor then intervenes.
- Find a friend and a buddy for the victim.
- Help her to improve her social skills and extend her group of friends.

- Find ways to help boost her self-confidence.
- Check back with the camper to ensure that the bullying has ceased.

The Bully

Consider bullying as a problem to be solved not as a crime to be prosecuted. The counsellor's role is to discipline not to punish. The goal of discipline is to instruct, guide and help the camper develop self-discipline; whereas, punishment leads to anger and further aggression.

- Find a private, quiet place to talk with the bully.
- Determine that the attack was deliberate. Help her to understand what she has done wrong and to accept ownership of the problem. The onus is on the bully to accept differences, not on the victim to remake herself.
- The bully needs to recognize and to consider others' feelings.
- Discuss ways to make things right and prevent the situation from recurring.
- Find a way to channel the bully's leadership abilities into something good. For example, if Alyssa invited Katie to a game of tetherball, they could enjoy an activity together where Katie's hyperactivity would not be annoying.
- Assist the bully to improve her friendship skills and to become a person who cares, shares, shows kindness and respect. A friend tolerates differences and doesn't try to change someone. She apologizes when she hurts another and treats everyone the way she would like to be treated. Camp is a great place to learn these valuable skills.

The Bystanders

- The bystanders need to understand that they have a
  responsibility to try to stop the bullying and to report the
  bullying incident to a counsellor.

Bullying should never be minimized or ignored. There are
too many cases where bullying in the extreme has resulted in
tragedy, either murder or suicide. The 1999 tragedy at
Colorado's Columbine High School of thirteen murders and two
suicides was the horrific result of years of taunting and bullying.
By confronting bullies at camp, we can help children grow up to
be caring, empathetic adults.

Complaints from parents

On a visitors' day, a camper's parents may come to you with a
complaint concerning their child. Their approach may be calm
or confrontational, depending on the seriousness of the issue. In
either case, your job is to be attentive, polite and respectful.
Listen to what the parents say without argument. Avoid making
excuses or taking a defensive stand. If there is a simple
explanation, offer it. Otherwise, reassure the parents that you
do take their concern seriously, that you will refer the problem
immediately to the director and that the parents will be hearing
from him.

Dealing with Really Serious Issues

14

It was the hardest thing I had ever done in my life. I had to tell my camper that she was going home – not because she had misbehaved or broken the rules or anything, but because her father was dying. Valerie knew before she came to camp that her dad was fatally ill. She also knew that if she was called home it was because his brain tumour was making it difficult for him to speak and he wanted his daughter near him while he could still talk to her.

Valerie's counsellor and her cabin mates didn't know what they could do to help. They hugged Valerie, wept with her and quietly helped her to pack. One camper handed her a *Seventeen* magazine, which had arrived with the previous night's mail, while another gave her some leftover tuck for the car ride home. They carried her luggage to the dock and waved goodbye. Sometimes all you can do is to be sad too.

One summer I had a great cabin of thirteen-year-old girls. Everyone got on really well. We had fun together all day. However, there was one problem, which surfaced at bedtime. One of my campers, Elizabeth, refused to lie down to go to sleep. It wasn't that she was a troublemaker; she just didn't want to go to sleep no matter how active we had been all day or how tired she was. Nothing I said or did would persuade her to lie down. Eventually I gave up. After taps, I said goodnight and left Elizabeth propped up on her pillow against the back cabin wall.

About two weeks into camp, I learned the reason. One quiet, moonlit night, walking back to the cabin from evening program, she shared a secret that only her immediate family knew. On the night of her grade eight graduation, she had been raped.

Sadly, some campers encounter tragedy in their young lives: physical or sexual abuse, the death of a mother, life with a depressive, suicidal father, a bitter divorce, a life-threatening illness or the loss of a close friend in a car accident. The director may have shared some of this sensitive information with you with the understanding that you will keep it confidential. Young counsellors are overwhelmed when presented with these tragic situations, especially if they themselves have enjoyed a sheltered, trouble-free existence. The best thing that you can do for your campers is quite simple. When they are ready to confide in you, you can listen with complete attention, empathy and sincerity.

You cannot change the past, but you can help your campers cope in the future. You can make sure that they have the best possible time at camp so that when they return home, they have enjoyed a brief respite and are a little stronger to face the problems in their lives.

After your campers have come to trust you, they may divulge some tragic information. Be wary of the question, "If I tell you something, will you promise not to tell?" There are some secrets that by law have to be revealed, such as physical or sexual abuse. You can support your camper by going with them to whomever they feel comfortable talking to – the nurse or the camp director (see Chapter 8).

It is highly unlikely that you will have to deal with such sad news, but during a child's stay at camp, there will be high points and low points. Part of your job is to teach your campers how to cope if necessary with disappointment or failure. If a canoe trip is cancelled because of bad weather, whining and complaining will

not help the situation. Acknowledge their disappointment; put it in perspective and make an alternate plan. If a camper does not pass his NLS, praise him for his effort, assure him he has learned something and encourage him to try again later. Lots of people don't reach a goal on the first attempt, but they have not failed unless they give up.

Separation and Divorce

On departure day, Jason sat at the front dock waiting for his father to arrive. He was worried because his dad was late. However, he was more concerned about something else. His parents had divorced two years ago. Just before camp, his father had remarried. The problem was, because his father was picking him up, was he taking him to a new house to live with him, his new wife and two stepsisters or was he going back to his old house to live with his mother? No one had thought to clarify this for him.

Counsellors need to be sensitive to children whose parents are separated or divorced. The issue may or may not arise depending on the recency of the event and how it was handled. Children are better able to accept the situation if they have been involved in open and honest discussions appropriate to their age.

If the subject arises, the counsellor can help by providing

- **reassurance**. "Your parents still love you…others have felt this way…you are not to blame."
- **acceptance**. "I understand that you are unhappy or angry, lonely, worried, resentful…it takes a long time to get over it, but it will get better."
- **stability**. Time spent in a safe, secure, happy camp environment will make him stronger to cope with the turmoil at home.

Disorders

Attention Deficit Hyperactivity Disorder (AD/HD)
Attention Deficit Disorder (ADD)
Obsessive Compulsive Disorder (OCD)
Tourette Syndrome (TS)

15

AD/HD, ADD, OCD and TS are interrelated behavioural problems that effect a small segment of the population. Nineteen to twenty-five percent of children with ADHD/ADD are also diagnosed as having a Learning Disability (LD). Living with one or more of these disorders can be devastating for a child and his parents. Children can experience poor self-esteem, low self-confidence, academic underachievement, poor social relationships, isolation, anxiety and depression. They may feel that they are stupid, crazy and unloved. Persons who do not understand these neurological disorders will observe a child's resulting behaviour and may conclude that he is delinquent, physiologically or emotionally disturbed, lazy or lacks parental control. However, with understanding and after the use of proper medication, these children can lead happy and productive lives.

Many camp parents may experience some anxiety when their child attends camp for the first time. As the following letter to the director illustrates, parents of a camper with a disability can be particularly anxious.

Susie is a very excited, happy, impulsive, young twelve-year-old. I hope you won't be offended if I remind you that she has trouble listening and following instructions easily. Also she is impulsive and has difficulty making friends. She is a very loving child who needs to be accepted and liked. If for some reason you feel that Susie is not settling in and is having a negative experience, please call and we will bring her home. She does not need to experience more failure in acceptance.

The good news is that children with these problems have a good chance for success at camp. They need a structured environment where the rules are clear, leaders are available, flexible and supportive and the activities are varied. Fortunately, unlike school, campers are not expected to sit still, listen and keep quiet for extended periods. These children are just as capable of learning as any camper, but they may need adjustments made to the teaching methods and environment. They are capable of making and keeping friends, but they need the help of an understanding counsellor to improve their social skills.

Recognizing these disorders

A camper with **Attention Deficit Hyperactivity Disorder (AD/HD)** may:

- ❑ act before thinking.
- ❑ begin an activity before instructions are complete.
- ❑ answer out of turn or before the question is complete.
- ❑ want things *NOW*.
- ❑ have difficulty following verbal or written directions.
- ❑ have difficulty predicting consequences.
- ❑ have difficulty waiting his turn in games.
- ❑ grab things from other campers.
- ❑ interrupt staff and campers and talk excessively.
- ❑ make careless mistakes.
- ❑ have difficulty remaining still or playing quietly.
- ❑ run and climb excessively and throw things.
- ❑ experience rapid mood changes.
- ❑ have a low tolerance for frustration.
- ❑ fidget, drum his fingers, shake his leg, tap his foot.

- ❏ feel angry.
- ❏ overreact to situations.
- ❏ move from one incomplete activity to another.
- ❏ be aggressive, immature or socially "clueless."
- ❏ have difficulty following rules of behaviour.
- ❏ lack problem-solving skills.

A camper with **Attention Deficit Disorder (ADD)** may:
- ❏ appear to lack energy.
- ❏ seem lazy and unmotivated.
- ❏ daydream.
- ❏ have difficulty listening, following instructions and finishing tasks.
- ❏ forget or lose things needed for activities.

Obsessive Compulsive Disorder (OCD) is characterized by involuntary, recurrent obsessions and compulsions that consume time, make the camper anxious and prevent him from functioning normally. Common obsessions are concerns about dirt, germs, illness, death and constant doubt. Common compulsions may include repetitive washing, cleaning, counting, checking and touching.

Tourette Syndrome (TS) is a tic disorder, which is a neurological condition composed of involuntary movements (motor tics) or sounds (vocal tics).
- ❏ The most common motor symptoms are eye blinking, head jerking and shoulder shrugging.
- ❏ The most common vocal symptoms are sniffing and throat clearing. Involuntary swearing occurs but is less common.

The symptoms often become more prevalent when the camper is under stress, anxious, angry, tired or excited. Asking a child to suppress tics produces stress.

It helps to know that:

- ❑ Children with these disorders may appear immature and function emotionally and socially at about 2/3 of their chronological age, i.e., a twelve-year-old acts more like an eight-year-old.

- ❑ These conditions occur more frequently in boys.

- ❑ Children with these disorders often cannot control their unpredictable, impulsive behaviour. They are not fidgeting, shouting, interrupting conversations and hitting their peers to be annoying. For the most part, they can't help it. Try to ignore negative behaviour. Don't criticize, blame or penalize campers for this involuntary behaviour. This does not mean they don't have to take responsibility for their actions. If a camper loses control and makes a mess, he still needs to help tidy it up. If he hurts another's feelings, he has to try to repair the damage.

- ❑ Things that the average camper takes in his stride can cause stress and anxiety in the child who is neurologically impaired (e.g., criticism in front of peers, insistence on eye contact, noise, crowds, surprises, being lightly touched, restrictions on movement or tasks that are too difficult). Be alert to your camper who is diagnosed with AD/HD in a noisy, crowded dining room or during all-camp events such as a Regatta. Allow him to withdraw temporarily from the situation.

- Don't insist on eye contact. Just because the child is not looking at you does not mean that he is not listening. A child may deliberately avoid looking to concentrate on listening.
- All the strategies for teaching and disciplining "typical" campers work equally well with campers who have AD/HD, ADD, OCD and TS. However, children with neurological impairments can be demanding and difficult and often need more time, patience and understanding.

Strategies to maximize social success

- With the permission of the camper and her parents, educate the cabin mates about the behaviours associated with the child's disorder. When cabin mates understand the problem, they will be less likely to tease and ridicule. Hopefully, the director will have placed the camper with cabin mates who are more inclined to empathize. An invisible handicap such as AD/HD is more difficult to understand than an external, visible handicap such as blindness or immobility.
- Discuss appropriate ways to deal with aggression. Teach your campers that it is better to fight with words than fists. It is best to move away and take time out before the situation gets out of control. Establish a safe place for the camper to go to regain control – somewhere quiet and private but where he is still supervised.
- Explain to the cabin the difference between fair and equal. What is fair is not necessarily equal. Fairness

means everyone gets what is needed not that everyone gets the same thing. For example, if one member of the cabin wears glasses, to make everyone equal that person should be asked not to wear glasses. Obviously this is not fair to the person with poor eyesight. Similarly, while the rest of the cabin is expected to remain seated through an entire meal, the camper with a hyperactive disorder should be allowed to get up and move around. Concessions should be made to allow the camper with hyperactive tendencies some legitimate activity during rest hour. To expect him to stay quietly in his cabin for an hour is asking for trouble.

❑ Learn to recognize the signs of impending loss of control (e.g., increased activity, raised voice, angry words) and allow the camper to take a break. Use humour to diffuse the situation.

❑ When a problem arises, don't automatically assume that the child with the disorder is at fault. Calmly ask questions to get to the truth of the matter.

❑ Help the camper to learn basic social skills. Encourage him to identify and name his own feelings, whether he is happy, sad, angry or scared. Help him to identify the cues that tell him how others feel by their facial expressions, choice of words or tone of voice. Help him with the answers to the questions:

• What can I do when I feel angry?
• What can I do when I feel rejected?
• What can I do when I want someone to listen to me?
• What can I do when I disagree with someone?

❑ Parents sometimes choose to take their children off their medications in the summer. However, in the best interests of the child, camp directors may persuade parents against taking a "holiday" from medication at least at the beginning of a session. On medication, the camper has a better chance of succeeding in establishing relationships with new friends at camp. Once the child who is neurologically impaired is accepted, he and his new friends may cope better with his changes in behaviour if he goes off his medication.

Strategies to maximize learning

❑ Position the camper close to the counsellor but still include the camper as part of the group.

❑ Minimize distractions.

❑ Assign a buddy to help the camper with tasks.

❑ Before beginning an explanation, call the camper's name to focus her attention and use an introductory sentence. "Elizabeth, I'm going to start explaining the game now."

❑ Speak slowly and clearly giving one direction at a time. Eliminate irrelevant information.

❑ Anticipate that the camper may misunderstand what you say. Ask the camper to repeat directions to ensure understanding.

❑ Permit the camper to ask for repetition. If possible, allow the rest of the group to get started; then, repeat the directions slowly for those who need further explanation.

❑ Provide lots of physical activity.

- ❑ Assign short tasks that can easily be accomplished and completed.
- ❑ Give the camper suitable warning before changing an activity.
- ❑ Encourage the camper to tell you before he gets frustrated, angry and out of control. "This is too hard. I don't know what I am supposed to do."
- ❑ If the camper is expected to learn a list of rules, provide a typed copy. Allow the camper to underline and highlight each rule or draw pictures to illustrate the rule.
- ❑ Create a supportive, stress-free learning environment where it is OK to make mistakes. When possible, ignore mistakes.
- ❑ Praise the camper no matter how small the success.

Campers struggling with neurological disorders do not want your pity. In fact, these campers can do wonderful things with their energy and creativity. What they do need, just like everybody else, is your love, understanding, support and patience. We would do well to heed the words of the Dalai Lama when he spoke of The Power of Compassion. He defined compassion as a developed sense of concern and respect – not pity – for others, a deep value necessary for being a human being.

Inclusion

*Connor asked his mom if his new day camp friend,
Gregory, could come over to play on the weekend.
After obtaining Gregory's home number from the
camp office, Mrs. Radcliffe made the arrangements.
When Gregory arrived on Saturday morning,
Connor's mom experienced an unexpected jolt. On
Monday morning, she called the camp office to
speak to the director. "You might have mentioned
that Gregory is blind," she said. The director
responded that if it was not important to Connor to
mention the fact then he saw no need to make a
point of telling the mother.*

It would be wonderful if we were all as accepting and casual as
Connor. To Connor, Gregory was a new friend who was fun to
play with. He saw Gregory's abilities not his disability.

Unfortunately, Rebekah's experience is more typical.
Writing in the *Globe and Mail*, she describes what it is like to be
a teenager in a wheelchair. "I have had to develop the mental
toughness to cope with the looks. I dream of the day when I can

go to school, go for a walk, go out for coffee or go shopping and not one person stares."

Instead of staring, Rebekah longs for someone to simply smile, wave or say hi. She yearns for people to look past her disability and treat her as a fellow human being.

It is no wonder that children with disabilities may have a reduced self-image. Too often, either they have been ignored or stared at, laughed at and called stupid, retarded or dumb. At camp, through inclusion, campers can learn to understand, accept and relate to children with disabilities. The similarities between people with disabilities and those without are far greater and more significant than the differences. Once everyone accepts this, children with disabilities will gain confidence and their self-image will improve dramatically. When counsellors accept children with disabilities, the rest of the campers will follow their lead.

The major obstacle to successful inclusion is fear. The camper with a disability fears failure and ridicule. Other campers may fear what is unknown and unfamiliar to them. Counsellors are afraid of being inadequate to meet the needs of all their campers.

How can you overcome these fears if a child with a disability is assigned to your group?

❑ In advance, learn all you can from the parents and the director about the child's disability and how he copes.

❑ Visit the camp or local library for appropriate books to teach yourself and your campers about inclusion.

Ask the librarian to help you make a suitable selection.

- *Don't Laugh at Me*, Steve Seskin and Allen Shambrin, Tricycle Press, Berkley, California & Toronto, 2002. This book, suitable for children ages four to eight, teaches tolerance to differences and respect for one another.
- *Andy and His Yellow Frisbee*, Mary Thompson, Woodbine House Inc., Bethesda, Maryland, 1996. The new girl at school tries to befriend Andy, an autistic boy, who spends every recess by himself spinning a yellow Frisbee.
- *My Brother Sammy,* Becky Edwards and David Armitage, Bloomsbury Publishing Plc., London, England, 1999. Sammy is special because he is autistic and like everyone else needs patience, acceptance and understanding.
- *Becky the Brave*, Laurie Lears, Albert Whitman & Company, Morton Grove, Illinois, 2002 is a story about epilepsy.
- *Sammy Sitstill,* Dr. Catherine Thompson, Crescent Publications, Toronto, 1999 describes how Sammy feels about Attention Deficit Disorder and what he does about it.
- *I'm Wendy Blair, Not a Chair*, Carolyn MacDiarmid, Canadian Council on Rehabilitation and Work, Toronto, 2002.
- *Our Brother Has Down's Syndrome*, Shelley Cairo, Annick Press Ltd., Toronto & New York, 1985.
- *Respect Is Correct*, Grossman & Bockus, S.S. Press 2002, teaches children to respect themselves and others.

- Treat the child with the disability as you would any other child. Don't hover or fuss. Don't draw attention to his disabilities. If the disability is not obvious or visible, the other campers may not even notice the differences. If the child with the disability misbehaves, discipline him the same as any other camper.
- The other campers in the group will copy how you relate to the child with special needs. You need to be patient, respectful, encouraging and positive.
- If the others ask questions, answer them as best you can. Coach cabin mates to ask their questions about differences sensitively.
- Focus on the camper's abilities and strengths rather than his limitations. Find opportunities for him to shine.
- With the child with special needs present, explain to the rest of the campers how they can help. "Timmy does not see well. We need to watch out for things that might harm him."
- Allow the child to do as much for and by himself as he is capable.
- Ensure success by assigning tasks that the camper is capable of achieving with some effort. Praise his success, then further challenge him with a slightly more difficult task.
- Assign a buddy to support and assist the child when needed.
- Recognize that sometimes the other children need a break from the child with special needs.

❏ The camper with a disability, as well as all campers, needs to be reassured that mistakes are OK. They are not a big deal. Everyone makes mistakes – including the counsellor! Mistakes are an opportunity for learning.

❏ Avoid elimination games where less capable players get removed first. Co-operative games allow everyone to continue having fun regardless of skill. Remark on the effort of the participants rather than the result.

❏ Take time at the end of the day for each camper to share accomplishments, achievements and successes. Encourage the campers to cheer each other on. Everybody 's self-concept will get a boost!

You're Special!

Pin a blank sheet of paper on each camper's back. Ask someone to pin a sheet on your back. Supply the group with felt markers. Invite the campers to write positive comments about their friends on the paper. After five minutes or so allow the campers to read the comments. A great image booster for everyone!

Nail in the Fence

Share with your campers the analogy of the Nail in the Fence. Every time we say or do something nasty or negative to someone, whether that person is able bodied or not, it is like pounding a nail into a fence. Later, if we realize our mistake and apologize, that would be comparable to pulling out the nail. But a hole still remains in the fence. No matter how much we try to right the wrong, the hole is still there. It does not go away. Our thoughtless words and our actions leave scars forever.

Tips for communicating with a camper with a hearing impairment

❏ Get the individual's attention with a wave or tap on the shoulder before you begin.

❏ Move away from background noise.

❏ Face the camper then speak slowly and clearly. Tell him the topic before beginning. Pause between statements.

- ❏ Speak in a normal tone of voice from a distance of between three to six feet. Don't shout.
- ❏ Include the person with the hearing impairment in the conversation. Speak directly to, not about, the individual.
- ❏ Keep paper and pencil handy to supplement verbal directions.

Tips for working with campers who are visually impaired

- ❏ Pair the camper with a sighted camper.
- ❏ When moving around, the camper who is visually impaired takes her buddy's arm not the reverse.
- ❏ In your verbal instructions, don't avoid using words like see or look.

Working with campers who have learning disabilities (LD)

A child with a learning disability may have an impaired ability to listen, think, speak, read, write, spell or do mathematical calculations. Fortunately at camp, teaching takes place with little emphasis on reading, writing, spelling or mathematics.

- ❏ Campers with LD need more time to learn. Don't rush them. Instructions should be simple, given slowly, repeated often and accompanied by visual aids and demonstrations.
- ❏ Campers with LD don't like surprises. Give ample warning and preparation before moving from one activity to another.

❏ Campers with LD tend to point out everyone else's mistakes. They may get into trouble and not understand why. A patient counsellor can help them to behave in a more socially acceptable manner.

As grateful parents describe in the letters below, when a child with a disability is successfully included into camp, miracles can happen.

Lauren made her first real friends at camp. One of Lauren's most vivid memories occurred when all the kids gathered around her in her walker on the soccer field to give her hugs when she kicked the ball. I cannot describe to you what that did for her self-esteem. Lauren loved camp and just believed it to be fun, yet she learned more in those few weeks than in many months at school.

Caleigh really enjoyed her camp experience. It gave her self-concept a big boost to be away from home and to achieve success in several areas – especially in "friendship-making."

Be prepared to be changed after working with campers with special needs. They will teach you about tenacity, tolerance, patience and perseverance. They will teach you to count your blessings and to embrace your life with gratitude.

Games and Programs

17

A well-prepared counsellor always has something fun to do when not much else is happening. While you wait for the bus to arrive, the program to start, the fire to burn down to coals for roasting marshmallows or the rest of the trip to complete the portage, play a game. You need a supply of **SANE** games –

Spontaneous **A**nywhere **A**nytime **N**o **E**quipment

I PACKED MY TRUNK

(suitable for young players)

⇨ Formation: sitting in a circle

⇨ The counsellor begins, "Hi, my name is Patti. When I packed my trunk for camp, I brought pyjamas. Who wants to tell us something they packed?"

The first camper to play repeats the statement and names an item. Unless he has played before, his item is not likely to fit the pattern, i.e., something with the same initial letter as his name. If the item does not follow the pattern, the counsellor says, "Sorry, but you can't bring that to camp." The counsellor then repeats, "Hi, my name is Patti. When I packed for camp I brought purple pants. Who else packed something for camp?"

The counsellor keeps giving clues until a camper realizes the pattern. As more campers perceive the trick, it will be easier for the rest to guess. If some campers are having difficulty, make it obvious by stressing the initial sound.

HOW MANY LEGS ON A HORSE?

⇨ Formation: scattered

⇨ Players: a dozen or more

The leader asks questions that require a numerical answer. How may sides in a triangle? How many stars in the Big Dipper? How many letters in "picnic"? Players rush to gather in groups of the correct number. The leader continues to call out questions and the players scramble to regroup. There are no winners and losers. The fun is in the quick pace, joining together then separating again.

LADDERS

⇨ Formation: Players in two equal lines face one another, sit on the ground with their legs together and stretched out so that they are touching feet with the player opposite. The pairs of legs look like rungs on a ladder. Leave sufficient room between the legs for players to step between easily.

⇨ Players: six to ten pairs

Each pair of players is assigned a number. When the leader calls a number, the two players stand up, run to the top of the ladder stepping carefully between each pair of legs, return behind the players to the bottom of the ladder, then run back up the ladder to their own position. The player sitting down in his original spot first wins a point for his team. Players forming the ladder must keep their legs still to avoid tripping the runners and injury to themselves. If played indoors, remove shoes. If played outdoors, step carefully!

The leader then calls another number. Numbers are called erratically to keep all players constantly on the alert.

STREETS AND ALLEYS

⇨ Formation: Players stand in equal rows with arms outstretched holding hands with the players in adjacent rows and two-arm-length distance behind the player in front.

⇨ Players: minimum of 18: four rows of four, one "It" and one "Chaser." With more players, there would be more rows making for a more exciting game.

⇨ Playing area: a large level space

The players form "Streets" by standing in rows with their arms outstretched and holding hands. "It" starts to run up and down the streets pursued by the "Chaser." Once the chase is on, the leader calls out "Alleys." On this command, all the players turn 45 degrees right and hold hands again. This forces "It" to change direction. He may not duck under arms. If unlucky, he may suddenly be face to face with the "Chaser." Allowing for some time for the chase up and down the Alleys, the leader continues to call "Streets" followed a short time later by "Alleys." On each command, the players turn 45 degrees right and form lines again with their arms outstretched. When "It" is caught, he takes a place in a row. The one replaced becomes the "Chaser" and the original "Chaser" becomes "It."

SHOE TOSS

⇨ Formation: circle

⇨ Players: six to twelve

One player removes one shoe. After making eye contact, he gently tosses his shoe to another player across the circle. That player then lobs the shoe to a different player. The toss continues until every player has been included and the shoe is tossed back to its owner. The sequence is then repeated making eye contact and tossing gently to avoid mishaps. If the shoe is dropped, simply pick it up and continue the sequence. A second player then removes his shoe and tosses it in the same sequence starting just after the first shoe. After perfecting a two-shoe toss, go for three or four shoes flying through the air simultaneously. The players will instinctively bend or stretch to avoid mid-air collisions.

Variation: Take a step back to increase the diameter of the circle and the challenge.

CAPTAIN'S COMING
⇨ Formation: scattered
⇨ Players: any number
⇨ Playing area: A large room or an open space becomes the boat. Designate the four walls or sides: one as the bow, the opposite as the stern, facing the bow to the right is starboard and to the left is port. The Crow's Nest is in the centre of the space.

Players respond to the command of the leader by running to the appropriate spot (bow, stern, starboard, port, Crow's Nest) or assuming the following positions:

⇨ Captain's Coming – stand at attention and salute
⇨ Submarines Sighted – lie on your back with one leg (periscope) straight up
⇨ Man Overboard – sit on the floor behind a partner and start rowing
⇨ Raise the Mainsail – stand, look up and move clenched hands in a rope-pulling motion
⇨ Officers' Mess – sit in a group of three or four and make an eating motion
⇨ Variation: Change the commands and actions to familiarize campers with the names of boat parts: thwart, keel, painter ring, mast, jib, etc.

MEMORY GAME

⇨ Formation: a circle

⇨ Players: any number

The leader displays ten to twenty items on the ground, which he has collected nearby (pine cone, stone, stick, leaf, etc.). The age of the players dictates the number of items and hence the difficulty of the game. He allows the group thirty seconds to memorize the items. The players then turn their backs to the collection and the leader removes one, two or three items and rearranges the others. On a signal, the group turns around and takes turns guessing which items have been removed.

ALPHABET SCAVENGER HUNT

⇨ Players: teams of three or four

Challenge the teams to search the surrounding area for ten minutes and attempt to find a natural item for each letter in the alphabet, e.g., acorn, birch bark, cedar branch, dragon fly, etc.

HUMAN KNOT

⇨ Players: an even number (12 – 20)

⇨ Formation: Begin standing in a circle shoulders touching.

Each player extends his right hand across the circle and takes the right hand of the player directly opposite. Each player then extends his left hand across the circle and takes the hand of a second person. This second person cannot be adjacent. Without letting go, the group unravels the knot by stepping over or ducking under clasped hands until they are back in a circle, facing either in or out.

CHAIN TAG

The person who is "It" catches a second person. The two join hands and run to catch a third. Three join hands and pursue a fourth player. Continue until everyone is linked in a chain.

SARDINES

⇨ Players: any number

⇨ Playing area: a large space with potential hiding places

While the players hide their eyes, "It" leaves the group and hides. After one minute, the rest of the players scatter and try to find "It." When a player finds "It," without alerting the others, he joins him in his hiding place. Play continues until all players have found "It" and are crammed like sardines in the chosen hiding place.

Pairs Challenges

CHICKEN FIGHT

⇨ Formation: players of similar size and height form pairs

Each player stands on his right foot with his left foot tucked behind his back held by his right hand. His left hand, behind his back, holds his right elbow. Hopping on one foot, each player tries to unbalance his opponent by bumping him with his left shoulder. The fight is over when one player's both feet land on the ground. The pair splits and each player challenges another "chicken."

TOUCH ME NOT

Two players stand facing one another slightly more than an arm's length apart. On a signal, each tries to touch the other, but at the same time is taking evasive action not to be touched. At all times, feet must remain stationary.

ARM LOCK CHALLENGE

Pairs of players sit on the ground, back to back, legs out straight with arms interlocked at the elbow. On the go signal, the challenge is to be the first pair standing without unlocking arms or placing hands on the ground.

Variations: attempt with three or four people

WHAT'S DIFFERENT?

⇨ Formation: Pairs facing one another
⇨ Players: any number of pairs

The pair faces one another and takes 60 seconds to thoroughly observe their partner from head to toe. The players then turn back to back and each player changes three things about their appearance, e.g., untie a shoelace, move a ring from the left to the right hand, turn back a sleeve cuff.

The players then face one another again and take turns identifying the changes.

The best games programs

- are run by enthusiastic counsellors who both lead and play with the campers.
- involve a maximum of participation and a minimum of sitting, waiting for a turn.
- allow campers to keep playing rather than being eliminated.
- require minimum organization, explanation and equipment.
- offer lots of variety – some active, inactive, familiar and original games.
- switch to the next game before campers become bored.

Games with minimal equipment

BLIND SQUARE
⇨ Equipment: a blindfold for each player and a length of rope (about 15 metres) with the ends tied together.
⇨ Formation: players begin in a circle, blindfolded, hanging onto the rope

The object of the game is for the group to form a perfect square without talking.

BARNYARD
⇨ Equipment: a blindfold for each player
⇨ Playing area: open area free of obstacles

Blindfold all participants and move them to a position about 3 metres from the next player. Making only the sound of a barn-yard animal (no talking allowed), the players gather together then line up by height.

CALCULATOR

⇨ Equipment: blindfold for each player
⇨ Playing area: a level area free of obstacles about 3 metres by 3 metres.
⇨ Number of players: about 15–20
⇨ Formation: scattered

Before play starts, whisper a random number in each player's ear using the numbers between one and the total number in the group. At the signal to start, the group forms themselves in numerical order without speaking.

Added challenge: assign some numbers higher than the number of players in the group and omit some numbers, e.g., assign numbers 1 through 25 to a group of 20 players and eliminate 6, 10, 13, 19, 24.

PICTURE CHARADES

⇨ Equipment: paper and pencil for each team
⇨ Formation: divide groups into teams of about 6. Each team forms a circle.

The leader has a list of the same 10 words for each team. The paper is folded so that only the first word is visible. A member of the team runs to the leader and reads the first word on the list. He rushes back to his team and draws pictures (no letters, words or numbers allowed) until his team whispers the word correctly (calling out the answer would spoil the fun for the other teams). A second player then goes to the leader who folds back the list to reveal the second word. The play continues until all ten words have been drawn and identified.

DRAGON TAG
- ⇨ Equipment: one scarf for each team
- ⇨ Formation: teams of 8–10 players standing one behind the other holding onto the waist of the person in front
- ⇨ Playing area: a large level space

Each team is a dragon. The first player is the dragon's head. The last player with a scarf hanging from his back pocket or tucked loosely into his waistband is the tail. On a signal, the head tries to catch the tail while simultaneously, the tail is taking evasive action to avoid being caught. When the head succeeds, he becomes the tail and the new head starts the chase.

Variation: One dragon chases another. Always holding on to one another, the head of each dragon tries to grab the scarf from the tail of the other dragons. If the head catches a tail, he returns the scarf to the head who moves to the back of his dragon and becomes a tail. Play continues.

KICK THE CAN
- ⇨ Equipment: a tin can
- ⇨ Playing area: a large space with places to hide
- ⇨ Players: any number

Place the can in the middle of the playing area. "It" stands beside the can. The rest of the players stand near the can. One person is chosen to kick the can as far as he is able. As soon as the can is kicked, the players scatter and hide. "It" retrieves the can and returns it to its original spot. "It" then looks for the hidden players. When he sights a player, he calls out his name and runs back and touches the can. If the discovered player can get back to the can first, he kicks it again and hides again while "It" retrieves the can. If "It" gets to the can first, the discovered player is captured and stands by the can. "It" keeps searching for the players. A hidden player can choose to come out of hiding before he is discovered, if he thinks he can get to the can and kick it before "It" spots him, calls his name and touches the can. This releases all captured players to hide again. Play ends when all hidden players are captured. A new "It" is chosen and the game continues.

When the weather is not co-operating

❑ Crank up your enthusiasm. Likely, you are more sensitive to the weather than your campers. Don't drag them down.

❑ Be sure that your campers are wearing suitable clothing.

❑ Stay active. If possible, with the proper clothing, play outside. If campers are allowed to sit around all day in the rain, they are sure to keep you up half the night!

❑ Spend lots of time with your campers to avoid homesickness or mischief.

Rainy Day Activities to do with your cabin group

- ❑ Invite another cabin group to join you for a party. Plan a theme and challenge them to dress up appropriately. Prepare a program of games, cards, songs or skits.
- ❑ Create a cabin crest with a suitable symbol for every person in the group.
- ❑ Write a cabin song to a familiar tune.
- ❑ Prepare a skit for variety night.
- ❑ Create hats to wear to dinner.
- ❑ Have a mud fight.
- ❑ Go for a Rubber Boot Hike.
- ❑ Go fishing.
- ❑ Organize an indoor tournament of board and card games.
- ❑ Host a talk show, a quiz show or a game show.

Trips Off Site

18

Whether you are leading an afternoon trip to the zoo or a canoe trip down the French River, you are now accepting the responsibility for your campers without the immediate support of the camp's senior and medical staff. Your director is confident that you can handle this responsibility or you wouldn't be going. He will expect you to make supervision and safety a top priority. Resist any temptation to relax the rules when you are out of sight of camp. Rather you should follow them more closely to ensure a safe and happy trip. Rarely will you be off site without a second leader to assist you.

A trip plan of your route is on file at the camp office. If for any reason you need to deviate from the pre-determined plan, you should notify the office of the change.

Take with you

- Phone numbers (camp and emergency services) and a cell phone or the correct change to make a phone call.
- A first aid kit appropriate to the length of the trip. It should include paper and pencil to record any treatment or medication administered while on the trip.

- Campers' medications with instructions on when, how much and how they are to be administered and possible side effects.
- A map and, depending on the nature of the trip, a compass. On canoe and hiking trips, the map should include locations of possible assistance if needed (roads, phones, stores to replenish supplies, hospitals, police stations, etc.).

Potential Problems

Missing Camper

When travelling with a group, along a city street, on a hiking trail or on a portage, position one staff person at the front and one at the rear. The campers, in buddies, are in the middle. Every member of the group stays within sight and calling distance. Constantly count your campers. On the lake, all boats stay within calling distance. The most senior staff person should be in the last craft.

Day campers should carry a card with the camp name and phone number and the correct change to make a phone call. Canoe trippers and hikers should carry a whistle.

If a camper is missing

- Ask the rest of the campers where the missing camper was last seen and gather information on why and where he might have gone.
- Take measures to keep the rest of the group safe. Search in buddies and wear a whistle for signalling.

Before starting, determine the signal to announce that the camper has been found or to call off the search.

- Search the last known location and the immediate area calling the person's name constantly.
- If the individual was last seen in the water or if there is reason to suspect that he may have entered the water, conduct an underwater search with all who are capable. A lifeguard oversees the search.
- Expand the search, always considering the safety and limits of the others in the group.
- If these efforts fail to find the missing person, report to camp as soon as possible with complete information about where and when the incident happened and a full description of the missing person.

Confrontations with wildlife

Wild animals are fun to observe – at a distance. Never approach or feed wild animals. Prevent your campers from touching animal bones. If they are curious, examine them using a stick.

Avoid bear problems

- Never store food in your tent.
- Store food in a pack hanging from the limb of a tree well away from your tents. Using a length of rope, hang the pack at least three metres off the ground and two metres away from the tree trunk. Don't store food under a canoe. You risk damage to the canoe as well as the loss of your food.
- Burn all flammable garbage. Scrape leftover food off your dish into the fire before washing. If fires are not

permitted, seal edible garbage in double plastic bags and hang with your food.
- Wash dishes immediately after a meal. Do not rinse or wash dishes in the lake. Wash in a pot and empty the waste water away from the site.

Bears are normally shy of humans and quickly run away, but if a bear wanders onto your site:
- Be aggressive. All of your party, standing in a group, should yell, throw sticks and rocks, make noise with pots and pans and wave their arms (to appear bigger) while allowing the animal a clear escape route.
- At night, shine flashlights into the bear's eyes to confuse it.
- Never stand between a mother bear and her cubs.
- If your aggressive attempts fail to frighten the bear, back away without running or turning your backs on the animal. As you retreat, drop a backpack or other object to distract the bear. Get into your canoes and leave the site.
- It is a myth that a bear will desist from attacking if you lie still and appear dead. Fight with every means that you have.

Rattlesnakes

Rattlesnakes will not strike unless threatened. If you leave them alone, they'll leave you alone. If you are in rattlesnake country, keep your eyes and ears open. Where possible remain on paths and out of tall grass. Always look before you step or reach into underbrush. Hiking boots and loose fitting pants offer the best protection. If you hear a rattlesnake (a loud buzzing), stop walking, locate the source of the sound, move away slowly and allow the snake room to escape.

If, despite your vigilance, someone is bitten, treat the situation as an emergency and ***seek medical help immediately***. There are only a couple of recorded deaths from bites and those victims did not get medical attention for days. The gravity of the situation depends on the weight of the victim (adults will tolerate a bite better than a child), where on the body the bite is located and the amount of venom injected. It is possible that, although a person is bitten, no venom or only a minimal amount has been injected.

- Speak reassuringly and urge the victim to remain calm.
- Keep the bite *below* the level of the heart.
- Keep the victim immobile. If possible, carry the victim or assist him to reduce activity. Lie him down while waiting for transportation. Remaining calm and inactive slows the circulation of venom through the body.
- Cleanse the wound.
- Remove any jewellery in the event of swelling.
- Do not apply a tourniquet or ice (cold changes the chemical nature of the venom and makes things worse).
- Do not cut the bite area or apply suction.

Although fatalities from rattlesnake bites are extremely rare, a bite can cause extreme discomfort and is best avoided.

Other Natural Hazards

- Learn to recognize poison ivy and teach your campers to avoid it. Poison ivy has three slightly drooping leaves, the middle one on a longer stem.
- Be wary of rotting logs that might house a wasp nest.
- Insist that campers wear shoes all the time for protection from sharp rocks or jagged sticks.

Poison Ivy

In a thunderstorm

- Get off the lake immediately.
- Move inland and find shelter – but not under the highest tree.
- Wear shoes.

Around the campfire

- Before lighting your fire, have a means of extinguishing it (sand or water) close by.
- Position your woodpile on the windward side of the fire.
- Keep campers at a safe distance, except those assisting with the cooking.
- Prevent campers from playing with or near the fire.
- Keep long hair tied back.
- Add logs carefully to avoid sparks.
- Remember that the rocks surrounding the fire are hot.
- If someone does get burned, immerse the burned area immediately in cold water.

- Extinguish your fire completely. It is safe to leave when you can touch the doused coals and surrounding rocks with your bare hands.
- Pitch your tents upwind and well back from the campfire.

Swimming

- All swimmers must be supervised by a qualified lifeguard.
- The lifeguard checks the area thoroughly for underwater hazards before the campers are allowed in the water.
- Specify the boundaries.
- Enter the water feet first. Do not dive.
- Campers always swim with a buddy.
- The lifeguard stands on the shore with a reaching assist (a paddle or lifejacket) and counts heads constantly.
- Swim in daylight only.
- Require weak swimmers to wear a life jacket.

If an accident happens

1. Remain calm.
2. Remove the victim from immediate danger and administer first aid.
3. Direct the assistant counsellor to care for the other campers.
4. Once the victim is out of danger, if possible and as soon as possible, contact the camp or the emergency services for further direction. Be prepared with details about the victim's condition and the exact location of the accident.

5. If the camp is out of communication, assess the situation in consultation with all other staff members. It is always better to err on the side of caution. If in doubt, evacuate. You have three choices:

   a) If speed is not an issue, the entire group moves for help together.

   b) If speed is a concern and the victim can be moved, a capable counsellor and another responsible person, possibly a mature camper, take the injured person to the nearest medical help. The second leader stays put with the rest of the group until the other counsellor returns.

   c) If the victim cannot be moved, the assistant counsellor and a second person, with complete information about the condition and exact location of the victim, go for help.

   d) As soon as possible, record all details of the event. (see Incident Reports, Chapter 7)

Sound Advice from the Experts

19

Experienced counsellors offer the following advice:

- *Don't sweat the small stuff.*
- *Be flexible.*
- *Don't impose your plan. Together with your campers, work out a plan.*
- *Listen to the kids. Learn their interests, then add them to the program.*
- *Play with, rather than compete with, your campers.*
- *Give 100%.*
- *Never stop trying.*
- *Set a good example.*
- *Know your limits.*
- *Teach campers to be safe.*
- *Pace yourself so that you still have energy at the end of the season.*
- *On your time off, get off the campsite for a complete break.*
- *Be prepared to work co-operatively with all kinds of people – most you will like; some you may not.*

Seasoned directors offer words of wisdom:

About your campers:
- *Truly like and care for each child. If a child is difficult, find out why. Then look till you find something likeable.*
- *Under everyone's hard shell there is someone who wants to be loved and appreciated.*
- *Put your campers first and you will feel great!*
- *Listen – really listen – and share.*
- *Never reject a gift from a child – no matter how humble the offering.*
- *Make your goal to duplicate the experience that you enjoyed when you were your campers' age.*

About your leadership:
- *It takes effort, thought and caring to be a great counsellor.*
- *Never be afraid to admit that you are having difficulty. Seek advice. If you don't know something, maybe an experienced camper has the answer. Ask him and give his ego a boost.*
- *Seek help from more experienced staff or the director. They will be flattered to be asked.*
- *Counselling requires complete commitment. Personal problems and distractions should not interfere with your responsibilities. Leave your emotional baggage at the door and pick it up on the way out.*
- *Know and adhere to all camp rules.*

Directors select counsellors because of their enthusiasm, confidence, energy, willingness and sense of humour. They know many of them lack counsellor job experience and expect to train and guide them. For the most part, directors are patient, tolerant, supportive individuals. They are willing to overlook innocent mistakes and correct errors. However, there are some behaviours that they find truly annoying, which you should resolve to avoid.

Directors are annoyed by:
- lazy counsellors, who sit and watch their campers at activities, then quickly jump to their feet when they see the director coming.
- gregarious counsellors who socialize till all hours and don't get enough sleep to be well-rested and ready for work in the morning.
- counsellors who take advantage and don't think the rules apply to them.
- counsellors who fail to complete their paper work (camper reports, letters to parents, self evaluations, program evaluations) on schedule.
- counsellors who forget that camp is all about the campers and not all about them.
- counsellors who talk among themselves about camp problems and politics within the campers' hearing.
- counsellors who allow their efforts and standards to slide as the summer progresses.
- counsellors who keep their campers waiting to start an activity.

When I asked a group of experienced directors the question, "Under what circumstances have you or would you fire a counsellor?" their answers were very similar:

- Drinking
- Drugs
- Dishonesty
- Theft
- Hitting a camper
- Putting a camper at risk

Each offence was a flagrant violation of the contract between the counsellor and the director.

A director needs a counsellor who is honest and trustworthy, someone who honours his contract and abides by all the rules even when no one is watching – both on and off site. He needs someone he can trust to represent the camp favourably on his time off. The public will make judgements about the camp based on your appearance and behaviour. If at any time during your employment you are tempted to break a condition of your contract, consider this: what part of the contract would you be willing to have your employer break? Would you be happy if he stopped paying you or stopped feeding you? I think not. Contracts are serious business. Your reputation rests on your signature.

Happy Endings

20

Final Days

You will need to be both well rested and well organized to give your campers 100% until your last camper departs on the final day of the last session.

In the days before departure, you will need time for the following tasks:

1. Check your campers' goals. If they are close to completing a goal or a level, encourage them to finish.
2. Gather their belongings (e.g., arts and crafts projects) from around camp.
3. Return all camp equipment.
4. Assist with packing.

When Mrs. Fraser opened her seven-year-old daughter's camp suitcase, she expected to empty the entire contents into the laundry tub. However, she was annoyed to discover that all the clothing was crumpled and shoved in carelessly. The contents were wet, smelly and covered in sand and dirt. On closer examination, she found that several items

*were missing. Mrs. Fraser concluded that the
counsellor had offered no help with her daughter's
packing and wondered how much time and interest
she had devoted to the rest of Allison's camp
experience. She immediately resolved to find
another camp for Allison the following summer.*

All campers need some help and supervision with their packing.
Younger campers need lots of help.

- Empty the luggage and dump out the accumulation of
  sand and dirt.
- Use the checklist to determine that all belongings are
  collected. Parents will tolerate the loss of the odd sock or
  underwear, but they expect most items to find their way
  home.
- Although the clothes are dirty, help your campers to fold
  them neatly.
- Hopefully the camper's soap is not in its original
  wrapper or the toothpaste unopened.
- The last thing to be packed at the last moment is any
  wet clothing in a plastic bag.

5. Send your camper home in the cleanest clothes available
    with a clean body and recently shampooed hair.
6. If your camp allows last-night pranks, give your group some
    guidance. It would be unfortunate to tarnish an otherwise
    wonderful experience with an inappropriate last-night
    prank. Most camps increase supervision to prevent such
    unfortunate occurrences.

7. As your campers depart, hand them a sealed envelope with the instruction printed on the outside: OPEN ON THE BUS (OR IN THE CAR). The note may recall some of the happy times shared and offer best wishes for the school year ahead and the possibility of a reunion in the city or next summer. You may want to include your address or email to keep in touch.

Send them home with a smile, a hug and a wish for the future. "See you next summer!"

Bibliography

Blackstock, Brian and Latimer, John, *Camp Counsellor's Handbook*, Methuen Publications, Agincourt, Ontario, Canada, 1984.

Burrow, David, *How To Be A Great Camp Counsellor*, McElroy Publishing, Shirley, Massachusetts, U.S.A., 1992.

Coloroso, Barbara, *The Bully, the Bullied and the Bystander*, Harper Collins Publishers, Toronto, Ontario, Canada, 2002.

Dornbush, Marilyn P., Ph.D. and Pruitt, Sheryl K., M. Ed., *Teaching the Tiger*, Hope Press, Duarte, CA 91009 U.S.A., 1995.

Gedatus, Gus, *Violence at School*, Capstone Press, Mankato, Minnesota, U.S.A., 2000.

Kindlon, Dan, Ph.D., *Too Much of a Good Thing*, Hyperion, New York, New York, U.S.A., 2001.

Leone, Daniel A., editor, *Anorexia*, Greenhaven Press Inc., San Diego, California, U.S.A., 2001.

Northway, Mary L. and Lowes, Barry G., editors, *The Camp Counsellor's Book*, Longmans Canada, Toronto, 1963.

Sheras, Peter, Ph.D., *Your Child: Bully or Victim? Understanding and Ending School Yard Tyranny*, Skylight Press, 2002.

About the Author

Catherine's lifelong love of camping began in 1953 when she accompanied her mother, Peggy Wells, the new camp cook, to Camp Tanamakoon in Algonquin Park. She remained at Tan until 1978 as a camper, counsellor-in-training, counsellor, Activity Head, Section Head, CIT and Program Director. On staff for fifteen summers, Catherine learned the art of counselling from an outstanding director and mentor, Elizabeth Raymer. Experience shared by other excellent camping professionals like Bruno Morawetz, John Latimer and Ron and Mickey Johnstone expanded her understanding and knowledge of camp leadership.

After five years as a teacher, in 1979, Catherine and her husband, George, purchased Camp Mi-A-Kon-Da for girls on Birch Island in Lake Wah Wash Kesh, near Parry Sound, Ontario. For twenty years, Catherine directed the staff and campers, George managed the business and property and the four Ross children enjoyed the benefits of summers at camp.

Catherine has held positions on the Boards of the Ontario Camping Association (OCA), the Canadian Camping Association /Association des Camps du Canada (CCA/ACC) and the Society of Camp Directors. Currently, she serves on the OCA Board as Chair, Educational Events. She is an Honorary Life Member of the OCA and has received OCA's highest volunteer recognition, the Dorothy Walter Award of Excellence. She is a recipient of CCA/ACC's Volunteer Recognition Award.

Catherine is past editor of *Camps Canada*, published by the CCA/ACC and the OCAsional News, the newsletter of the Ontario Camping Association. She has published two books, *When the Wilderness Beckons* (1979), a canoe-tripping handbook, and *The Mi-A-Kon-Da Story* (2004), a camp history. Her articles on camping have appeared in Toronto's *City Parent* and *Canadian Living*. Several American magazines have printed her children's camp stories.

Notes